MINI

CROATIA

How to download your Free eBook

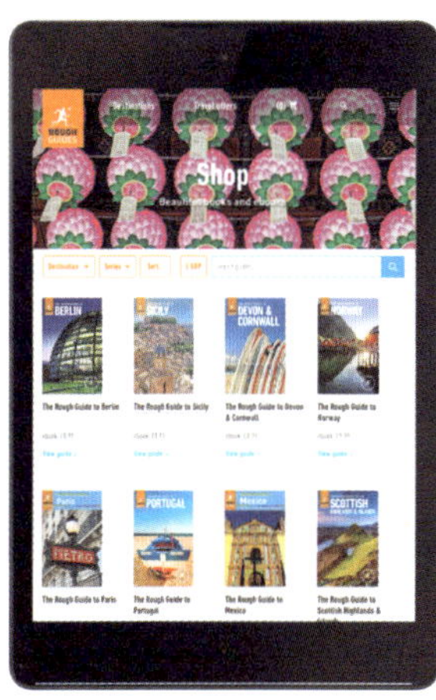

1. Visit **www.roughguides.com/free-ebook** or scan the **QR code** opposite

2. Enter the code **croatia928**

3. Follow the simple step-by-step instructions

For troubleshooting contact: mail@roughguides.com

Samsonite

Contents

6 **Introduction**

14 10 Things not to miss
16 A perfect tour of Croatia
18 Croatia for foodies
20 Island-hopping around Croatia

22 **History**

35 **Places**

35 Zagreb
44 Inland Croatia
50 Istria
61 Kvarner Gulf
68 Dalmatia

91 **Things to do**

91 Outdoor activities
95 Shopping
100 Nightlife
102 Croatia for children
102 Festivals and events

104 **Food and drink**

122 **Travel essentials**

142 **Index**

Introduction

Croatia may be one of Europe's newest nations, gaining its independence from Yugoslavia in 1991, but even before its role in *Game of Thrones* it was one of the world's most alluring tourist destinations. A member of the European Union since 2013, Croatia's small size is deceptive, at just 56,594 sq km (21,845 sq miles). An incredible variety of scenery is packed into this boomerang-shaped country, from the magnificent 1,778km (1,105 mile)-long coastline, to the sweeping limestone mountains and endless fertile plains of the interior. Croatia's identity has been shaped by its position at a political and ethnic crossroads, across the Adriatic from Italy, and bordered by Slovenia, Hungary, Serbia, Bosnia-Herzegovina and Montenegro.

A natural playground

Croatia's most dramatic natural attraction is its Adriatic coastline, which sweeps from Slovenia in the north to the Montenegrin border in the south, taking in 1,246 islands, islets and reefs en route. Crystal-clear water and countless rocky bays and sandy coves lure visitors and locals alike. In summer the climate is glorious, with hot sunny days tempered by a cooling sea breeze. Even in the spring and autumn the mercury usually rises high enough for T-shirts and shorts.

Away from the beaches, high-rise mountain ranges offer opportunities for hiking, climbing and extreme sports. Further inland there is the UNESCO World Heritage Site of Plitvice Lakes National Park, a limestone

NOTES

UNESCO has listed ten World Heritage Sites in Croatia: Dubrovnik and Trogir old towns, Diocletian's Palace and medieval Split, the Plitvice Lakes, the Euphrasian Basilica, Šibenik Cathedral, Stari Grad Plain on Hvar Island, the *Venetian defence walls* and a series of medieval tombstones scattered across the country.

Sunset in Šibenik

oasis of gushing streams, pounding waterfalls and green-hued lakes. Perhaps less visited by tourists, but in its own way just as impressive is the Krka National Park in Dalmatia, with a series of lakes and streams plunging inexorably towards the Adriatic in a dramatic passage through the karst backbone of the country.

Croatia's varied landscape also makes it highly attractive for sports enthusiasts. It is a popular destination for sailing, with countless yachts cruising around the islands. Sailors are catered for by chic restaurants and hotels that are a far cry from the faceless concrete blocks that kicked off Croatian tourism in the 1960s.

The sailors flocking to the fifty plus marinas that dot the coastline have been joined by scuba divers. Conditions are excellent for diving, with a range of sites suitable for divers of all levels. The island of Biševo with its famous Blue Grotto is every bit as alluring as its Italian counterpart in Capri, and around the neighbouring island of Vis there are at least a dozen shipwrecks suitable for diving.

Cities and towns

While Croatia has eight national parks, its towns and cities also hold plenty of interest. Zagreb, the capital and most populous city, is a large, modern metropolis complete with high-class hotels, richly stocked museums and restaurants that reflect its cosmopolitan nature. To the south, the Austro-Hungarian architectural and political influences of Zagreb and Varaždin give way on the coast to Venetian and Roman remnants.

Split, Croatia's second-largest city, is a chaotic, sprawling centre built on the shores of the Adriatic with its core contained within the 2,000-year-old Diocletian's Palace. This World Heritage city-within-a-city is bursting with bars, cafés and boutiques that emit a decidedly Mediterranean buzz. Croatia's depth of history comes

WHAT'S NEW

The euro and Schengen In 2024 Croatia joined the euro and Schengen zones. While the latter brought an end to queues at the country's borders, the former has been blamed for significant price rises of almost everything.

Pelješac Bridge The new bridge spanning the Adriatic between the 'mainland' and the Pelješac Peninsula is a godsend for motorists who no longer have to pass through a tiny sliver of Bosnia (two passport controls and long queues were the norm) to get from the northern part of Croatia to Dubrovnik.

Michelin stars In 2024, a Croatian restaurant in Rovinj called *Agli Amici Rovinj* became the first to receive two Michelin stars.

New luxury hotels At least seven new luxury hotels are set to open along the coast in 2025, with Pula, Split and Sisak set to benefit.

E-ferries The main ferry company Jadrolinja has announced it will be introducing electric ferries on some lines in 2026.

The falls at Skradinski Buk, Krka National Park

from centuries of conflict in which the Greeks, Romans, French, Venetians and Hungarians have all vied for control. The legacy of this eclectic past is evident in world-class attractions such as the 2,000-year-old Roman Arena in Pula and the mosaic-embellished Basilica of Euphrasius in Poreč, another World Heritage site. It also surfaces when you least expect it, when a Venetian bell tower emerges above an insignificant town or when you come upon

BLUE FLAG BEACHES AND MARINAS

Croatia may not have many of the fine sandy beaches that you find in Italy and Spain, but it does have some of the cleanest beaches anywhere in Europe. In 2025, there were 74 Blue Flag beaches dotted along the coastline and hemming the islands.

Dubrovnik, one of the most beautiful cities in Europe

an arrow-straight thoroughfare that has been smoothed over by Roman sandals.

Croatia also has its own home-grown architectural highlights such as Šibenik and, the most striking town of them all, Dubrovnik. Nicknamed the 'Pearl of the Adriatic' by Byron, this stunning city-state has been immaculately preserved in its original Baroque glory. Walking around Dubrovnik during the renowned summer festival and savouring the sun melting into the Adriatic from the city's ramparts are unforgettable experiences.

A Split personality

The locals of Zagreb and Split live very different lives that hint at the contrast between the two main cultures in Croatia: the Central European order and rationality of the north and the more laid-back lifestyle of the coast, where the steamy summer days slow things down. There is a rivalry that ripples through the nation with stereotypes aplenty. Bring the Serbs of Krajina, the Bosnians of the border areas and the Slovenian influences of the northwest into the mix and more contrasting lifestyles emerge, with the varying ways of life coexisting today in relative harmony.

The legacy of the war

Scratch the surface anywhere in Croatia and you will hear people talking openly about 'the war'. Images of a burning Dubrovnik and helpless refugees filled TV screens across the world in the early 1990s. However, the reality is that, except in a few places such as Vukovar and Knin, it is hard to tell that the bitter conflict ever burned through the country. Indeed, it is perhaps the years of communism combined with the Homeland War that have kept

WHEN TO GO

Croatia has a Mediterranean climate on the coast, with warm summers and mild winters, and continental inland – slightly hotter during the summer, and extremely cold in winter. July and August constitute the peak season on the Adriatic, and this is definitely the time to visit if busy beaches are what you're looking for. Inland cities tend to be quiet at this time. Accommodation soon fills up at the height of summer, and it may be more relaxing to travel in June or September, when there is less pressure on facilities. Autumn is a good time to enjoy inland Istria and national park areas like the Plitvice Lakes and the River Krka. Given the innocuous winters on the Adriatic coast, urban sightseeing in historic centres such as Zadar, Split and Dubrovnik can be more enjoyable at this time. Winters inland are a world away from the coastal climate: it can even snow at higher altitudes. Advent markets in Zagreb add spice to the pre-Christmas season. Spring is well into its stride by mid-March: warm, dry weather makes this a great time for outdoor activities.

Sixth-century mosaics in the Euphrasian Basilica

Dubrovnik, its riviera and Croatia's other treasures unspoilt for so long. It is only when you make a conscious effort to search for clues that the scars emerge, such as differently coloured roof tiles and deserted villages of burnt-out houses; there are even some bullet holes that remain in the walls of Dubrovnik's old town. However, for Croatians under 30, citizens of the EU, members of the Schengen zone and users of the Euro, the Homeland War is ancient history.

Croatia today

Croatia has made rapid progress in putting itself on the map since independence, not least with international sporting successes (see page 30). Tourism expanded rapidly as tour operators of all sizes rushed to offer everything from villa and beach holidays to sailing including luxury overnight boating trips, hiking and other adventure tours. Croatia's tourist numbers have also been boosted by the growth of budget air-travel routes and the expansion of the national motorway network.

Croatia's post-war progress was partially put on hold by the controversial right-wing president Franjo Tuđman, but after his death in 1999 the country was welcomed into the global fold. In July 2013, Croatia became a member of the European Union, and in 2024 it entered the Schengen and Euro zone. From a war-torn, former Yugoslav republic, Croatia has become one of the most visited tourist destinations in the Mediterranean, and rightly so.

SUSTAINABLE TRAVEL

Overtourism In summer, Croatia manages to disperse half of central Europe along its coast but some places (Dubrovnik, Hvar Town) are showing the strain. Try seek out lesser-known spots for a more enjoyable experience or visit off-season.

Stay green and local It's not difficult to stay local in Croatia with many accommodation options being family-run apartments or agritourism facilities. To see how green your accommodation might be, visit www.responsibletravel.com.

Greensail Sailing is an eco-friendly way of exploring the Croatian islands. Green Sail (www.green-sail.com) promotes green marine tourism by teaching potential boat operators and captains how to sail sustainably.

Buy local Croatia makes some of the Adriatic's finest foodstuffs such as olive oil, truffles and lavender. In places like Istria and Hvar, buying direct from producers supports the local economy.

Water During the summer months, some of Croatia's islands have a water problem which is only exacerbated by millions of tourists. Throughout Croatia try to use water conservatively.

Greenwashing Many local businesses are faced with sustainability targets they simply cannot meet and this leads to greenwashing. Don't shy away from giving honest online reviews if you see any examples.

1

2

3

10 Things not to miss

4

5

6

1. **BASILICA OF EUPHRASIUS IN POREČ**
   The mosaics here are superb examples of Byzantine art. See page 56.

2. **DUBROVNIK**
   This stunning city has been dubbed the 'Pearl of the Adriatic'. See page 79.

3. **RAB TOWN**
   A quintessential coastal town is found on the island of Rab. See page 67.

4. **TVRĐA**
   The old quarter of Osijek has fine Baroque architecture. See page 49.

5. **ROMAN AMPHITHEATRE IN PULA**
   Once known as Polensium, the city is home to Croatia's top archeological site. See page 51.

6. **DIOCLETIAN'S PALACE**
   A remarkably intact Roman complex in Split. See page 76.

7. **PLITVICE LAKES NATIONAL PARK**
   Comprises a chain of sixteen lakes linked by waterfalls. See page 47.

8. **MLJET NATIONAL PARK**
   With two stunning lakes, Mljet in Southern Dalmatia reflects the beauty of Croatia's coastline. See page 89.

9. **PAKLENICA NATIONAL PARK**
   Popular for climbing and hiking. See page 65.

10. **ST DONAT'S**
    This cylindrical church is one of several fine places of worship in Zadar. See page 70.

A perfect tour of Croatia

DAY 1

Pula. Fly into Pula and wander around the magnificent Roman amphitheatre. Treat yourself to an overnight stay at the *Valsabbion*, where you can admire the panoramic rooftop views.

DAY 2

Opatija. En route to Opatija, take a detour to explore the medieval hilltop town of Motovun and sample the local truffles. In Opatija, admire the grand villas along the seafront and enjoy coffee and cream cake at a Viennese-era café.

DAY 3

Zadar. Stay overnight in Sukošan. Head to Zadar in time to see the sunset and the sound and light show. Enjoy the entertainment at the *Garden* or *Arsenal* nearby.

DAY 4

Šibenik and Krka Falls. Spend the night in style on one of Croatia's smallest islands, Krapanj. On your way, take lunch in delightful Šibenik and visit the Šibenik City Museum. Then head for the magnificent Krka waterfalls.

DAY 5

Trogir. Take the coast road to Trogir, stopping at picture-perfect Primošten. Watch the superyachts go by as you enjoy a pizza on Trogir's Riva, and explore the UNESCO-protected old town. Then head past Split airport to join your skippered yacht in Marina Kaštela.

DAY 6

Hvar. Cast off and take a peek at the proud grandeur of Diocletian's Palace from Split's bay, before making for a deserted anchorage on the Pakleni Islands, near Hvar. Take an afternoon swim before heading off to Hvar Town for an evening exploring its nightlife and history.

DAY 7

Korčula. Sail to Korčula town and spend the day in one of Croatia's most stunning medieval cities. Pick up some fresh fish and local delicacies for dinner on board the next day. While in town, dine in style and enjoy the incredible views on the terrace of the extremely fashionable (and expensive) *Lešić Dimitri Palace*.

DAY 8

Mljet. Take your time sailing between the Pelješac Peninsula and Mljet Island, perhaps stopping off for a relaxing bathe or swim in Mljet's salt-water lakes. Anchor off the northeast coast of Lokrum Island to watch the city lights of Dubrovnik while feasting on fresh fish on board.

DAY 9

Dubrovnik. Disembark in Dubrovnik and walk the city walls before getting a taxi to the airport. If you have time, go first to nearby Cavtat and take a diving trip to discover some of Croatia's many Greek and Roman relics, or simply relax over a late lunch at one of the city's seafront restaurants.

Croatia for foodies

DAY 1

Zagreb. The capital is home to the best of Croatia's well-established gastro-bistro culture, with a growing number of small, creative restaurants. Typical cuisine includes Austro-Hungarian dishes such as goulash and pancakes as well as the local speciality *štrukli*.

DAY 2

Inland Istria. Good home cooking is very much the rule in inland Istria whose cuisine is very similar to that of Italy, but with many a Slavic and central European addition. Seek out local truffles grated sparingly over homemade pasta.

DAY 3

Rovinj. This tourist magnet has a great seafood scene. Try *brodet*, a rich fish stew, and sample fresh oysters from nearby Lim Fjord (see page 58). Wineries outside the town offer Teran red wines.

DAY 4

Volosko. Some of the Adriatic's best restaurants are squeezed into this seaside village, with freshly-caught fish and delicious local scampi the standout choices (see page 118).

DAY 5

Skradin. Located where the River Krka meets the Adriatic, Skradin offers the best of both coastal and inland Dalmatian cuisine, with a mouth-watering array of unique local recipes.

DAY 6

Mali Ston. There's something special about eating oysters and mussels mere metres away from where they were harvested, and Mali Ston is the best place to do it. Red wines from nearby Pelješac vineyards are irresistible (see page 111).

DAY 7

Pag. The barren island of Pag to the south of Rab is known for one thing – cheese. Produced locally from sheep's milk, this is a hard, dry cheese known for its saltiness. This is down to the local sheep grazing on salty vegetation, the salt in question carried inland by the wind. Every restaurant worth its salt (!) offers the cheese and it can be bought across Croatia.

DAY 8

Split. This large city has become something of a mini foodie destination in recent years. The dish to try here is *pasticada*, a rich, slow-cooked beef stew marinated in vinegar and spices, then braised with prunes, red wine and vegetables, and traditionally served with gnocchi.

DAY 9

Dubrovnik. Dubrovnik's signature dishes are black risotto (cuttlefish ink risotto) and *rožata* – a popular custard pudding similar to the French crème brûlée, flavoured with rose liqueur (rozulin), giving it a delicate floral aroma (see page 104).

Island-hopping around Croatia

DAY 1

Krk Island. Start in Krk, Croatia's largest island, connected to the mainland by a bridge near the city of Rijeka. Explore the medieval town of Krk, taste Vrbnička Žlahtina wine in Vrbnik and swim in crystal-clear bays. Visit Baška for its sandy beach and distracting views of the mountains on the mainland.

DAY 2

Cres and Lošinj. Take a short ferry to Cres, a rugged, quieter island known for Lake Vrana and the picturesque Cres Town. Cres is linked to Lošinj by a tiny bridge across the channel that divides them. Lošinj is known for lush vegetation and its friendly dolphin population. Stop off in Mali Lošinj for some local seafood.

DAY 3

Rab Island. Return north slightly to Rab, renowned for its sandy beaches – rare in Croatia – and the elegant Rab Town with its four distinctive bell towers. Stroll the old town and sample the famous Rab cake (*Rapska torta*), an almond-based dessert (see page 118).

DAY 4

Pag Island. Head south to Pag, known for its barren landscapes and culinary specialties like Pag cheese (*paški sir*) and lamb. The town of Pag boasts unique lace-making traditions (see page 97), while Novalja is a summer noisy nightlife hotspot.

DAY 5

Brač. Continue south to Brač, home to the iconic Zlatni Rat beach in Bol and the white limestone used in Diocletian's Palace (see page 8).

DAY 6

Hvar. Take a boat across to Hvar (see page 86), a bit of a party island but one also known for its lavender fields, stylishly steep Hvar Town and the UNESCO-listed Stari Grad Plain. The hard-to-reach beaches on the southern coast of the island are truly dream-like.

DAY 7

Korčula. Next up is Korčula, reputedly the birthplace of Marco Polo. Korčula Town resembles a mini-Dubrovnik with its medieval walls. Try local wines like Grk and Pošip, and traditional dishes such as *žrnovski makaruni*, a hand-rolled pasta.

DAY 8

Mljet. Stop at Mljet, a tranquil, forested island boasting a wonderful national park with saltwater lakes and a Benedictine monastery on an island in Veliko Jezero lake (see page 89). Ideal for cycling, swimming and kayaking.

DAY 9

Dubrovnik. The town obviously isn't an island, but it is the ideal transit point for lots of them, including Lokrum Island and the Elaphiti Islands.

History

Delving into the complex history of one of Europe's youngest nations throws up as many unresolved questions as answers. Croatia has been an independent nation on only three occasions: during the reign of the Croatian kings in the tenth and eleventh centuries, during World War II, though it was essentially a Nazi puppet state, and since 1991 after its bitter separation from Yugoslavia. Most Croats today have always felt a strong sense of national identity despite previously being labelled as Yugoslav on their passports. All this makes gleaning unbiased historical information from within the country a tricky task.

Statue of Ban Jelačić on the main city square, Zagreb

From prehistory

Thanks to the discovery of 'Krapina Man' and his Neanderthal kinsmen in the Zagorje region (see page 44) in the nineteenth century, it has been possible to trace habitation in Croatia to 30,000 BC. The hilltop settlement where the remains were found, near the small town of Krapina, is one of the most important prehistoric sites in Europe. Along the Croatian coast there is also a scattering of evidence that hunter-gatherers may have settled in the region at least twenty thousand years ago.

Greeks, Romans and Byzantines

By the time the Greeks arrived on the island of Vis in the fourth century BC, a smattering of tribes known as the Illyrians inhabited both the coastal areas and hinterland. From 229 BC onwards the Romans moved into the region, rapidly swallowing up large chunks of the country and beginning their makeover by building solid roads and structured towns, and imposing their way of life. The amphitheatre in Pula (see page 51) dates from this period, as does Diocletian's Palace in Split (see page 76). Many other reminders of Roman heritage can be seen in Croatia today.

NOTES

The Roman emperor Diocletian was probably born in Salona (near Split). Upon retirement in around AD 300, he returned to his roots and built a vast palace, which still stands today.

The Romans continued to hold sway over the region until the western part of their empire collapsed in the fifth century. For a short time, the Ostrogoths ruled Croatia, before the eastern part of the Roman Empire, known as Byzantium, gained control of Istria and Dalmatia. The dominance of the first few centuries of Roman rule never truly returned, with persistent threats from both the Illyrians and the Asian Avars.

Croatia's kings

The Croats are widely thought to be a Slavic people who came to the region in a mass migration from the plains to the north. Their Slavic cousins, the Serbs and Slovenes, are also thought to have moved to the area around this time. As more Croats arrived, their influence grew and they acquired their own king, Tomislav, a heroic character still revered in Croatia. In securing the Croatian state in 925, Tomislav saw off both the Venetian Republic and the Hungarians. Following the end of Tomislav's reign in 928, a succession of kings took their turn as the Croatian monarch, but Tomislav remains the symbolic hero.

It was during this period that Croats began converting to Christianity. Recognition by the Pope in the ninth century marked their allegiance to the Roman rather than the Byzantine Church. Grgur (Gregory) of Nin, a Slav bishop, tried to establish a Croatian national church, championing the use of an alphabet called Glagolitic and the performance of Mass in the vernacular. However, the Latin clergy defeated his attempts.

Coveted by Hungary and Venice

An agreement in 1102 confirmed Hungarian control over most of Croatia, although the Croats were allowed a degree of autonomy and their own representative *(ban)* and parliament (*sabor*). The Hungarian involvement in Croatia continued for many centuries. In the first three they faced persistent threats from the Ottoman Empire to the east. The fear of the Islamic 'hordes' underpinned the way Budapest viewed Croatia. Across the country's rugged interior, a series of fortifications (*krajina*) were spread out as a bulwark against the Ottomans, a barrier that was ultimately successful, but often teetered on the verge of being overrun.

As Hungary secured much of inland Croatia, the Venetians moved in to snatch swathes of coastline, over which they took control in 1420. During this time Dubrovnik was one of the few places to retain its independence. The Venetians, like the Romans centuries earlier, brought in their own architectural ideas and town plans, leaving an indelible impression on the Croatian coast that lingers to this day in fortified towns, fine buildings and elegant church bell towers. The Venetian hold was always tenuous, based more on securing trade routes than acquiring and governing territory, and they faced persistent threats not only from the Ottomans but also from pirates such as the infamous marauders of Senj.

The fall of the Divine Republic

As the eighteenth century ended, the French, under Napoleon, finally triggered the end of the Venetian Republic in 1797. Among the booty they collected were the Venetian possessions along the Croatian coast. The history of Napoleon's 'Illyrian Provinces' was to be short-lived after the French defeat at the hands of Russia in the winter of 1812–13. The Austro-Hungarians were on hand to pick up the pieces and the Treaty of Vienna confirmed their gains in 1815.

Despite, or perhaps because of, spending centuries under the will of various powers, Croatian identity and patriotism started to reassert itself in the first half of the nineteenth century. The result was that Josip Jelačić, a popular army officer from the Vojna

Dubrovnik was once an independent republic called Ragusa

Krajina, became *ban* (governor) of Croatia, though he was careful to pledge loyalty to the Habsburg Empire. This drive for recognition manifested itself most strongly in the cultural and linguistic fields, and it came at a time of similar Serb and Slovene risings in what evolved into a pan-Slavism movement.

World Wars I and II

The dissolution of the Austro-Hungarian Empire that was precipitated by World War I presented an ideal opportunity for this pan-Slavism to become something more solid, with the formation of the Kingdom of the Serbs, Croats and Slovenes in 1918 (known as Yugoslavia after 1930). Despite high hopes and official talk of unity, many Croats were disappointed to find that, instead of the loose federalism they had anticipated, much of the real power shifted to Belgrade.

When Germany swept into Croatia in April 1941, extremist members of the Ustaše Party, under Ante Pavelić, seized the opportunity and collaborated in the setting up of a Nazi puppet state. The war brought out the worst in some Croats, and Pavelić and his cronies established a concentration camp at Jasenovac where Serbs, Jews and other 'undesirables' were murdered (see page 48). This sorry chapter in Croatia's history ended in 1945 with Tito's communist partisans taking control of Yugoslavia and massacring thousands of Ustaše forces and collaborators.

Croatia under Tito

Tito (born Josip Broz, 1892–1980), himself a Croat, kept a tight rein over Yugoslavia during his four decades as president and Communist Party leader. Croatian nationalism was suppressed, as were nationalist sentiments in Bosnia, Serbia and Kosovo, though they still simmered below the surface. Economic resentment grew in Croatia from the 1960s when mass tourism started bringing in substantial amounts of hard currency, which was often siphoned away from the coast to swell central government coffers in Belgrade.

The disenchantment helped to fuel desires for greater self-government, which manifested itself in the Croatian Spring. This involved reform-minded politicians and intellectuals, some of whom called for Croatian to be recognized as a separate language from Serbian. The Croatian League of Communists was split between those who wanted to keep the status quo and those looking for greater autonomy, a tension that was expressed in student riots in the early 1970s. Seeing the unity of Yugoslavia threatened, Tito moved in to clamp down on the Croatian Spring, with sackings and forced resignations in December 1971.

Memorial at the site of the Jasenovac concentration camp

Ethnic rivalries and the descent to war

While Tito had been largely successful in suppressing the worst of the ethnic rivalries within Yugoslavia, he had been less successful in grooming an heir. His death in 1980 created a power vacuum and a sense of instability that ultimately paved the way for the bloody Balkan wars of the 1990s. In the absence of Tito, the Yugoslav presidency was left to a rotating collective, representing the republics.

Amid political wrangling and machinations, the then little-known Serbian politician Slobodan Milošević emerged to assert Serbian nationalism and endorse the view that Belgrade was not interested in letting the various parts of Yugoslavia enjoy an amicable separation. As moves towards independence took hold in Slovenia and Croatia, many Serbs, including Milošević, realised that dissolution was inevitable and instigated a plan that involved setting up a 'Greater Serbia' by swallowing large sections of the other parts of Yugoslavia.

Statue of the president of former Yugoslavia, Josip Broz Tito, in his birthplace, Kumrovec

Tensions finally reached a head in June 1991 when Slovenia and Croatia declared their independence. An ex-Yugoslav general, Franjo Tuđman, was at the helm of a new Croatian nation, which was not officially recognized by the United Nations and which faced the immediate danger of the Serbs within its borders combining with the powerful Yugoslav Army to cut off parts of its territory and claim them for 'Greater Serbia'.

The Homeland War

From June 1991 onwards, the fighting escalated rapidly as the rebel Serbs and the Yugoslav National Army (JNA) outmanoeuvred the poorly armed Croatian police and guard units to 'ethnically cleanse' swathes of Croatia. Milošević gambled on a quick victory before the international community became involved, but the rapid Serb successes in central Croatia were halted in Slavonia by the defiant stand of the people of the eastern city of Vukovar. This city stood on the border with Serbia and bore the brunt of heavy shelling and air raids as it became cut off and a siege of medieval ferocity ensued. Vukovar's resistance was echoed in the south by Dubrovnik, which was also besieged. Both cities became patriotic symbols of Croatian resistance.

NOTES

Slovenia declared independence from Yugoslavia on the same day as Croatia – June 25, 1991. However, with far fewer ethnic Serbs among its population and with no history of ethnic cleansing, it did not provoke the savage reaction from Serbia that Croatia drew.

Although Vukovar did eventually fall and Serbian forces committed further atrocities to those that had already scarred their military advances around the country, Zagreb was never threatened. Serb military progress soon slowed as the Croats managed to gather hardware and personnel together for a more organized defence. In the spring of 1992, soon after Germany had unilaterally recognized Croatian independence, UN units were deployed as a buffer between the two sides following international negotiations.

The peace deal froze the battle lines and promised to return territory to the Croatians, but the vague timescale did not satisfy Tuđman. His government continued to acquire military equipment

THE SIEGE OF DUBROVNIK

The siege of Dubrovnik was the most publicized of a series of attacks from the Yugoslav Army and it was the one that led news programmes around the world. The city had no particular strategic value nor any real Serb claim of ownership (the Serb population was around seven percent), but it was surrounded by a naval blockade and shelled from the surrounding hills for seven months, its fifty thousand inhabitants trapped behind the medieval city walls. By the end of the siege, more than five hundred historic buildings had been damaged and 43 citizens killed.

in a period when the rebel Serbs had lost the backing of the Yugoslav Army. In 1995, the Croatian 'Flash' (May) and 'Storm' (August) offensives may have incited the ire of the UN, but the Croats rapidly regained much rebel Serb territory. In 1998, as part of the Erdut agreement, the last tracts of Slavonia, including devastated Vukovar, were handed back to Croatia and the Homeland War was at an end.

With the establishment of the International War Crimes Tribunal for the former Yugoslavia at The Hague, various notable indictees were gradually brought to trial, though two prime culprits, Tuđman and Milošević, both died before being sentenced. Charges of war crimes against Croatian forces and national heroes provoked fury among many Croats, but the country did make made steps to co-operate with the tribunal, with the arrest of General Ante Gotovina in Spain in 2005. Sentenced to prison in 2011, he was acquitted by appeal in 2012. The tribunal's final judgement was issued in November 2017 and the institution formally ceased to exist on December 31, 2017, partially closing this chapter of Croatia's history.

Modern Croatia

As one of Europe's newest nations Croatia has quickly established itself on the world stage, not least in its sporting achievements since the millennium. Goran Ivanišević became the first wildcard entry to win Wimbledon in 2001, and the national tennis team became the first unseeded winners of the Davis Cup in 2005. In 2002, Janica Kostelić won Croatia's first three Olympic gold medals in skiing and a gold and silver in Turin in 2006. Her brother, Ivica, won two silvers at the 2010 Toronto Games. The Croatians were runners-up in the World Men's Handball Championship of 2009. In 2016, Valent and Martin Sinković won gold medals for rowing at the Olympics in Rio de Janeiro; they repeated their success at the Olympics in Tokyo in 2021. Also in 2021, Mate Pavić and Nikola Mektić triumphed in the men's doubles at Wimbledon and won a gold medal at the Olympics in Tokyo, becoming the first Croatian Olympic tennis champions. However, the cherry on the sporting cake came in 2018 when Croatia's football team beat England in the semi-finals of the FIFA World Cup, only to lose to France in the final.

Life under siege in Dubrovnik, 1991

Croatia's emergence on the political and economic stage has been slower, in part because of President Franjo Tuđman right-wing policies and abrasive style, which marred the country's image abroad in its early years. Since his death in 1999, Croatia has been welcomed back into the international community and foreign investment has grown substantially. The government demonstrated its determination to enhance Croatia's profile by its

Kolinda Grabar-Kritović, Croatia's first female president

improved co-operation with the War Crimes Tribunal at The Hague.

The country was still plagued by corruption, however, and the imprisonment of former Prime Minister Ivo Sanader in 2012 was a low point. But Croatia's concerted efforts to clean itself up were rewarded with long-awaited EU membership in 2013. Following Kolinda Grabar-Kitarović's five-year term as Croatia's first female president, leftist Zoran Milanović, a former Prime Minister, was elected to power in 2020. Croatia completed its rehabilitation into the international community in 2023 when it adopted the euro and entered the Schengen zone. Tourist revenues for 2024 were the highest ever and many infrastructure projects have come to fruition in recent years.

Chronology

30,000 BC 'Krapina Man' evidence of prehistoric settlement in Croatia.

229 BC–AD 600 Roman then Byzantine empires hold sway.

925 King Tomislav becomes the first king of an independent Croatia.

1102 Hungarian control over Croatia agreed.

1420s Venetian Republic occupies much of the Croatian coast.

1797 Venetian Republic collapses to Napoleon.
1918 Kingdom of Serbs, Croats and Slovenes proclaimed.
1929 Fascist Ustaše set-up under Ante Pavelić.
1941 German troops invade and Ustaše collaborates in establishing the Independent State of Croatia (ndh).
1945 Tito's Partisans enter Zagreb, marking the start of Communist rule. Tito is declared prime minister of the new Yugoslav Federal Republic.
1990 Moves towards Croatian independence led by Franjo Tuđman.
1991 Declaration of independence; Croatian Serbs revolt with the backing of the Yugoslav military. The Homeland War breaks out. Fall of Vukovar marks nadir of the war.
1992 United Nations brokers a ceasefire.
1995 Croatian 'Flash' and 'Storm' offensives regain much Serb territory.
1998 Last occupied areas returned to Croatia through the UN.
1999 Death of President Tuđman.
2005 The arrest of alleged war criminal Ante Gotovina signals the opening of serious negotiations for EU membership.
2009 Croatia joins Nato.
2013 Croatia joins the European Union.
2015 Kolinda Grabar-Kitarović becomes the first female Croatian president.
2017 The International War Crimes Tribunal for the former Yugoslavia at The Hague is officially closed on December 31.
2018 The Croatian men's national football team reaches the FIFA World Cup final. They eventually lose to France 4–2.
2020 The COVID-19 pandemic sweeps Croatia, causing a national lockdown and school closures.
2021 Croatia celebrates its 30th anniversary of independence.
2023 Croatia adopts the euro and enters the Schengen Zone.
2025 Tourism numbers break all previous records.

St Mark's Church in Zagreb, the capital of Croatia

Places

Most of Croatia's tourist industry is concentrated on the Adriatic coast, in Dalmatia and the Istrian peninsula, including the numerous islands. International airports serving the coast include Dubrovnik, Split, Zadar, Rijeka and Pula. A motorway system (www.hac.hr) connects most of the country's main cities and runs along the coastline. This is a big improvement on the scenic but often slow and serpentine coastal road, the Jadranska Magistrala (Adriatic Highway). Island-hopping is a great way to experience coastal Croatia; the main ferry company is Jadrolinija (www.jadrolinija.hr).

Inland Croatia also has plenty to interest visitors, including the lively capital Zagreb, impressive mountain scenery, castles, spas and the outstanding Plitvice Lakes National Park. From Zagreb, the *autocesta* (motorway) runs east to Slavonia.

Zagreb

Highlights

- **Donji Grad**, see page 36
- **Trg bana Josipa Jelačića**, see page 38
- **Kaptol**, see page 39
- **Gornji Grad**, see page 40
- **Novi Zagreb**, see page 43
- **Parks and gardens**, see page 43

A charming old quarter, a number of museums and leafy parks and a lively nightlife make **Zagreb** ❶ an ideal city-break destination. Many people heading for the coast tend to bypass the capital and in doing so miss out on this compact, lively metropolis, whose younger residents give it a buzz that is particularly evident in its myriad cafés on a balmy evening. Be aware, however, that the city dwellers too tend to head for the coast in the summer months, during which time the super-heated capital becomes abnormally quiet. The city skyline is set to change dramatically in the coming years, with a number of office skyscrapers approved for construction. In March 2020, the city suffered a major earthquake which left one person dead and 27 more injured; many historical buildings in the city centre also suffered damage and some attractions remain closed.

Donji Grad

Spreading north of Glavni Kolodvor, the central railway station, is Donji Grad (Lower Town). Standing proud in Trg Kralja Tomislava, the square opposite the station, is the equestrian **statue of King Tomislav** Ⓐ, the first of the Croatian kings, his commanding figure a symbol of the city and meeting point.

North of the central railway station is a string of neatly tended squares, often filled with students reclining on benches and older citizens idling by the fountains. Trg Kralja Tomislava is home to the **Art Pavilion** (Umjetnički Paviljon; www.umjetnicki-paviljon.hr), an Art Nouveau building housing temporary exhibitions. At the time of writing, it is still closed to the public due to damage caused by the 2020 earthquake.

The next park north is Strossmayer Trg, containing the **Strossmayer Gallery of Old Masters** Ⓑ

NOTES

The Zagreb Card represents good value if you plan to spend more than a couple of days in the city. Choose from 24 or 72 hours. Holders are entitled to free admission to four major museums and the city zoo, reduced admission in many galleries and museums, free public transport, and theatre, restaurant and nightclub discounts. The card is available from the tourist information office on Trg Bana Josipa Jelačića and most Zagreb hotels. See http://zagrebcard.com for more details.

The Art Pavilion

(Strossmayerova Galerija; temporarily closed following the 2020 earthquake). It was commissioned by the eponymous Slavonian bishop in the nineteenth century and has a collection of works by Italian masters including Tintoretto and Veronese. Look out also for the Baška Tablet, said to be the oldest example of Croatian Glagolitic script, brought here from its original home on the Kvarner Gulf island of Krk.

A few blocks west, in Trg Maršala Tita, is the **Museum of Arts and Crafts** **C** (Muzej za Umjetnost i Obrt; www.muo.hr; charge), designed by the Austrian architect Hermann Bollé, whose name pops up all over the city, including the Mirogoj Cemetery (see page 43). The eclectic collection includes ceramics and furniture, clocks, silverware, glass and religious art. Next-door is the grand, neo-Baroque architecture of the Croatian National Theatre.

WHERE TO SHOOT THE BEST PICTURES

It would be impossible to list all the best photo-worthy spots in Croatia, so we'll mention a select few. **Split** offers the lively Riva waterfront, as well as Diocletian's Palace with its unique tangle of Roman and medieval remains, and the green oasis that is Sustipan Park, perched on a cliff above the water. The old fishing port of **Rovinj** is a favoured location for photographers on the Istrian peninsula, as is the magnificent city of **Pula** with its impressive architecture and beautifully preserved mosaics.

Diagonally opposite the museum, facing Rooseveltov Trg, is Zagreb's most impressive museum; the **Mimara** **D** (Muzej Mimara; www.mimara.hr; temporarily closed due to the consequences of the 2020 earthquake, due to reopen in 2026), housed in an old grammar school. The artists represented include Raphael, Caravaggio, Rembrandt, Rubens, Van Dyck, Velázquez, Gainsborough, Turner, Delacroix, Renoir, Manet and Degas. There have been persistent mutterings from certain sections of the art world about the dubious authenticity of some of the work, but if you take it on face value the four-thousand-strong collection is impressive. The contents were donated to the city by Dalmatian collector Ante Topić Mimara and also include archeological finds from around the Mediterranean.

A brief detour along Savska cesta will take you to the Nikola Tesla Technical Museum (www.tmnt.hr; charge) and its collection of historic machinery including planes and automobiles.

Trg bana Josipa Jelačića

The epicentre of Zagreb life, **Trg bana Josipa Jelačića** **E**, is surrounded by grand nineteenth-century buildings. The statue of the viceroy, Ban Josip Jelačić, erected in 1866 and banished by Tito in 1945, has been returned to its prominent position at the heart of this plaza. Today, the square is the best place to take the pulse of the city.

Kaptol

The Kaptol district breaks away uphill from Trg Bana Josipa Jelačića. Without doubt, the highlight here is the neo-Gothic **Zagreb Cathedral** F (free) with its twin bell towers, designed by Hermann Bollé. Unfortunately, in March 2020, the cathedral suffered in the earthquake with one of its spires breaking off. Reconstruction was well underway at the time of writing. A religious building has stood on the site since the reign of the Croatian kings in the tenth century and it is still a place of devotion for many local residents. Notable features include a series of thirteenth-century frescoes that have survived the cathedral's numerous traumas, including a

Trg bana Josipa Jelačića, the central square of Zagreb, sets the pace of the city

devastating earthquake in the nineteenth century. The cathedral is also the last resting place of the controversial Croatian clergyman Archbishop Stepinac (d.1960), who was accused of colluding with the Nazi puppet regime during World War II, but is considered a martyr by many Croats. Look out for Ivan Meštrović's relief of Christ with Stepinac. Until the completion of the Dalmatia tower in Split, this was the tallest building in Croatia.

A short walk west from the cathedral is **Dolac Market**, where locals head to source fresh fruit, flowers and vegetables. A sprinkling of bars and restaurants overlook the small market square, providing a good view of the action. If you're planning on catching a train from Zagreb to Budapest, Vienna or the coast, the market is a good place to stock up on provisions, if you get there before 1pm.

Angel on Zagreb Cathedral

Gornji Grad

The oldest part of the city is Gornji Grad (Upper Town), which still retains some of its historical charm. You can reach it by walking up from the cathedral, but it is more fun to take the funicular from Donji Grad. At the top is the **Lotrščak Tower** G (Kula Lotrščak; charge), where an art gallery with a modest array of paintings for sale is a prelude to the main attraction – a sweeping view of the city from the observation level, accompanied at noon by loud cannon blasts.

St Mark's Church roof detail

Just north of the tower is one of Zagreb's most intriguing attractions, the **Museum of Broken Relationships** (Muzej prekinutih veza; www.brokenships.com; charge). Stories of love lost and found are told through objects donated by people around the world, and the result is poignant and compelling.

Below Lotrščak Tower, **Strossmayer Promenade** (Strossmayerovo šetalište) offers similarly fine views of the city spreading across the plain, with its main buildings, including the cathedral, clearly visible. The most intriguing bench from which to savour the vista is the work of modern artist Ivan Kožarić, with the bronze figure of the writer Antun Gustav Matoš awaiting someone to share the view with him.

A short walk north brings you to **St Mark's Church** (free). This striking church features a multi-coloured nineteenth-century roof, upon which the Croatian coat of arms is clearly visible. The church itself dates back to the thirteenth century, though there have been many major renovations over the centuries. Inside are several works by Ivan Meštrović, including a sinewy depiction of Christ on the cross in typically challenging Meštrović style.

Fans of the twentieth-century cult Croatian sculptor will not want to miss the **Atelier Meštrović** H (http://mestrovic.hr/atelijer-mestrovic; charge), just north of St Mark's. Meštrović lived here from 1924 to 1942 and the displays of his original sketches and plans illuminate many of the works that can be seen around Zagreb, including the *Crucifixion* in St Mark's Church and the statue of *Grgur of Nin*, outside Diocletian's Palace in Split, with a replica in Varaždin.

Mirogoj Cemetery

Further north, the **Zagreb City Museum** I (Muzej Grada Zagreba; www.mgz.hr; charge) features, among other displays, scale models that help visitors to understand the different phases of the city from medieval times to the modern day.

In the shadow of Gornji Grad is **Tkalčićeva** J. This cobbled thoroughfare is lined with pavement cafés and on busy nights it is packed with people out to see and be seen. There are so many cafés and bars to choose from that the best option is to simply stroll along its length a couple of times before you settle down and order your coffee or an Ožujsko, the excellent locally brewed lager.

Novi Zagreb

South of the Sava river, the urban post-war sprawl is brightened by Zagreb's **National Library**, **Lisinski Concert Hall** and, most impressively, by the **Museum of Contemporary Art** (Muzej Suvremene Umjetnosti; www.msu.hr; charge). This enormous space contains more than five thousand works displayed, including a large film and video collection.

Parks and gardens

Zagreb's green spaces provide a welcome escape from the bustle of city life on a hot day. West of the station are the **Botanical**

MIROGOJ CEMETERY

The Mirogoj Cemetery (free) is the place to be if you are dead in Zagreb. Here, in one of Europe's grandest graveyards, the city's richest residents and luminaries vie for space.

A local joke makes fun of the fact that many of the deceased inhabitants of Mirogoj have far more impressive abodes than the actual living inhabitants of the city, and there is more than a little truth to this. The cemetery was built in 1876, the majority of it the work of Hermann Bollé, whose extravagant tastes and designs are evident both here and elsewhere in the city. The entrance is particularly striking: an elegant neoclassical facade draped in ivy with a colonnade and a row of four lime green cupolas topped off with one large central dome.

It is worth spending some time admiring the sculptures and grand tombs that grace the interior. Look out too for the memorial to the victims of the Homeland War, with a monument inscribed with the names of 13,500 dead, situated just outside the main gate.

There are regular buses from the cathedral to Mirogoj Cemetery.

Gardens (Botanički Vrt; http://botanickivrt.biol.pmf.hr; charge), established at the end of the nineteenth century. About ten thousand species are packed into small confines, surrounded by paths and benches, and one of the pools is home to carp and a colony of terrapins.

Maksimir Park is only a short tram ride 3km (1.86 miles) east of the city centre and spreads out across 128 hectares (316 acres). Despite plans to build a new facility, both the national football team and local side Dinamo Zagreb play their home games at the slightly outdated sports stadium facing the park. The atmosphere during games can be rowdy, but there is no better venue to see both Croatian patriotism and the local citizens' love of Zagreb expressed so vehemently. Within the park boundaries are **Zagreb Zoo** (https://zoo.hr; charge), a boating lake and walkways, as well as plenty of shady trees.

Lake Jarun is also only a short tram ride from the city centre, 4km (2.48 miles) to the southwest. As well as an artificial lake suitable for swimming, sunbathing and water sports, there are cafés, restaurants and bars that are open day and night in summer.

Inland Croatia

Highlights

- **North of Zagreb**, see page 44
- **Plitvice Lakes**, see page 47
- **Slavonia**, see page 47

North of Zagreb

Varaždin ❷ is the only large town in the **Zagorje** region, which extends north of Zagreb towards Hungary and Slovenia. Zagorje is a hilly green playground for the citizens of Zagreb, who come to visit the chocolate-box castles, relax in the spas and sample the local food and drink. A good sweep of Zagorje can be covered in a long day trip from Zagreb, but to get a real feel for this rewarding region it is worth basing yourself in Varaždin for a few days. The region is best visited in spring or in late autumn when temperatures are lowest and when there's most life in the streets and villages.

Trakošćan Castle

Varaždin's old town, which is more than 800 years old and for a brief period was Croatia's capital city, is being smartened up. The city's main tourist attraction, its stunning **castle**, is on the UNESCO World Heritage 'Tentative List'. The fortifications date back to the twelfth century and in the sixteenth century the castle was an integral part of an attempt by the Austrian Empire to fend off the attentions of the Ottomans. When the threat of Ottoman invasion ceased, the local Erdödy family bought the fortress and transformed it into a grand home. Today, it houses the **City Museum** (Gradski Muzej Varaždin; www.gmv.hr; charge).

Varaždin's Fortress is one of a string of castles that spread out over Zagorje, set amid the rolling hills and forests that characterize the landscape. One of the most appealing is **Trakošćan Castle** (www.trakoscan.hr; charge), less than an hour's drive west of Varaždin, and another popular excursion from the capital. A castle has stood on the site since the sixteenth century, but the

Plitvice Lakes National Park

one that is open to the public today is largely the result of a rather fanciful nineteenth-century remoulding. The castle is worth a few hours' exploration to see the various collections (weapons, art, books, furniture), as are the surrounding grounds where a small lake has a path running around its shores and a café by the water's edge. Also on the UNESCO tentative list is **Veliki Tabor** (www.veliki-tabor.hr; charge), a ruggedly impressive castle dating back to the twelfth century.

The Zagorje region gained a reputation as a spa retreat in the nineteenth century when visitors from Austria would come to take the waters. Of the spas left today, **Krapinske Toplice** (www.krapinsketoplice.com) has one of the best. There are a number of pools of varying temperature, from lukewarm to steaming hot, where you and the family can join in the relaxed fun.

Plitvice Lakes

The **Plitvice Lakes National Park** ❸ (NP Plitvička Jezera; www.np-plitvicka-jezera.hr), 110km (68 miles) south of Zagreb on the old road to Split, is one of Croatia's top attractions and was added to UNESCO's World Heritage list in 1979.

Whatever the season, the beauty of Plitvice is immediately evident. The fresh, clear waters rush through a network of sixteen lakes and tumble-down waterfalls stretching for some 8km (5 miles). You can visit the lakes on a day trip from Zagreb or from the southern cities and resorts, but it is best to spend a night at one of the hotels inside the park boundaries. Wildlife within the park includes otter and deer, the venomous nose-horned viper and even bears, not to mention a wide variety of fish and birds.

Getting around Plitvice could not be easier, as electric boats and tourist trains connect the trails and wooden walkways. Hopping on and off the boats and traversing the wooden walkways as the spray of the waterfalls mists all around is a big part of the fun.

In high season, do not be deterred by the crowds: set off early in the morning and head south to Lake Proščansko, which is usually quiet and peaceful all year round. Often the best plan is to divide your visit into at least two adventures: one to the remote upper lakes and another to the more popular lower lakes, avoiding the temptation to cover everything too quickly. Sadly, swimming in the lakes is not allowed.

Slavonia

The oft-neglected eastern region of Slavonia has plenty to offer, not least the fact that it is never overrun with tourists. However, as in Zagreb you may find most of the population has escaped to the coast in July and August. It is just a three-hour drive east along the *autocesta* (motorway) from Zagreb.

The city of **Osijek** ❹ is a good base for exploring the area and sampling the excellent wines, with a growing number of wine tours and cellars to visit. It is also close to **Kopački rit Nature Park** (http://pp-kopacki-rit.hr), one of the biggest areas of remaining intact wetland in Europe, providing a broad range of tours and activities. However, 35km (22 miles) along the trunk road from the *autocesta* to Osijek it is worth stopping off at the small town of **Đakovo** to visit its exquisite cathedral, whose twin towers can be seen long before you arrive in town. The neo-Gothic Basilica of St. Peter, built between 1866 and 1882, was commissioned by the Croatian clergyman Bishop Strossmayer. A sculpture of Strossmayer sits gazing back towards the monumental building from across the road. Đakovo also has a Lippizaner horse stud farm (https://ergela-djakovo.hr/en/) originally established in 1506.

Osijek was subject to savage Serb attacks during the Homeland War, but the city has since regained its verve, helped by a young student population and a lively café scene along the River Drava. The core of the city is blessed with some impressive architecture, most notably on Europska Avenija, which has a collage of Art Nouveau buildings. Bishop Strossmayer commissioned the massive Cathedral of St Peter and St Paul, built in neo-Gothic style at

JASENOVAC CAMP

Jasenovac is a name that stains the twentieth-century history of Croatia and one that continues to cause controversy today. The World War II concentration camp that was built in the woods southwest of Zagreb on the way to Slavonia had thousands of Serbs, Jews and other 'undesirables' put to death amid savage conditions. Much debate in the 1970s and 1980s focused on how many hundreds of thousands were killed here, but these squabbles are just a background to the brute fact of the camp's existence. Serbian forces occupied Jasenovac during the Homeland War and many of the surviving objects were removed. A Memorial Museum (www.jusp-jasenovac.hr; free) tells some of the horrifying stories of the victims.

the end of the nineteenth century.

A ten-minute stroll from Europska is **Tvrđa**. This old quarter was neglected for decades and the Serbs shelled it heavily in the early 1990s, but efforts to shore up the roofs have revived the area. The Catholic Church has also spent much time and money resurrecting the exteriors and interiors of the many churches housed within the old walls. Tvrđa was originally built by the Habsburgs as a bulwark against the Ottoman Empire and its rich history is only now starting to be unearthed.

Church in Tvrđa, Osijek's old quarter

Vukovar ❺ is a name that conjures up a whole range of emotions in any Croat. It had been a pleasant Baroque town on the Danube inhabited by a mix of Croats, Serbs, Bosnians, Germans and Slovaks among others. Tragically for Vukovar it lay on the eastern edge of the new Republic of Croatia, and in 1991 the political leaders in Belgrade conspired with local Serbs to 'ethnically cleanse' the town. Its devastation was one of the lowest points of the Homeland War. The Vukovar water tower stands as a lasting memorial to what the city endured.

Visiting Vukovar today gives a real sense of what happened to Croatia during the war – something that is not easy to appreciate in the coastal resorts. The remaining residents soon dispel any doubts about whether it is distasteful to visit the town. They are only too happy to see outsiders who take an interest in the suffering that they feel was ignored by the rest of Europe. Tourism has been crucial to the recovery of Vukovar and, on a larger scale, to Slavonia and the Vukovar Municipal Museum and the Vučedol Culture Museum (http://vucedol.hr), are both worth a visit.

Istria

Highlights

- **Pula**, see page 51
- **Vodnjan**, see page 53
- **Rovinj**, see page 53
- **Poreč**, see page 56
- **Other coastal resorts**, see page 56
- **Boat trips from the coastal resorts**, see page 58
- **Istrian interior**, see page 58

JAMES JOYCE

James Joyce fans may want to follow the trail left in Pula by the great Irish writer before he flitted north to Trieste and set about finishing *A Portrait of the Artist as a Young Man* and embarking on his epic *Ulysses*. The local authorities have always been keen to promote the minimal Joyce connection, and the former local branch of the Berlitz language school where he found work in 1904 is now open as the *Uliks (Ulysses) Café*. Outside the café is a bronze sculpture of Joyce sitting at his favourite chair, with his trademark hat and walking stick. The sculpture was designed by local artist Mate Čvrljak and it has become almost obligatory to have your photo taken with the author.

Not that Joyce was all that enamoured with Istria. In a letter from Pula dated 1904, he described Istria as 'a long boring place wedged into the Adriatic, peopled by ignorant Slavs who wear red caps and colossal breeches'.

Istria ❻, the triangular-shaped peninsula that extends into the Adriatic in the far north of the Croatian coast, is one of the country's most popular tourist destinations. Since the 1960s, visitors have been pouring into the purpose-built resorts in and around Vrsar, Umag, Novigrad and, of course, Poreč and Rovinj. The Homeland War did not directly affect Istria, and tourism has always been a mainstay of the local economy. Interesting places to stay here include the *agroturizams*, old farmhouses that have been turned into small hotels and guesthouses.

The Roman Amphitheatre in Pula

Istria's largest city is Pula, whose fine amphitheatre is a reminder of the time when the Romans held sway over the peninsula. Their empire left numerous traces in Croatia, and the central cores of both Pula and Poreč are still built on the original Roman plan. The Venetians, too, left their mark on Istria, most notably in the coastal town of Rovinj and in the interior, where Venetian fortifications are the legacy of the days when pirates and Ottomans threatened the trade routes and the Istrian peninsula.

Pula

Croatia's Roman heritage is most impressive in **Pula**. The city's dramatic legacy from its days as Polensium is the **Roman Amphitheatre** (www.ami-pula.hr; charge), standing proud near the waterfront. Originally, the amphitheatre would have attracted 23,000 spectators to its bloody entertainment; today it is still pulling in the punters for rock and classical concerts and its annual film festival. In fact, the summers months, but especially July and August, are typically full of events. A small museum is housed in the vaults, but the main attraction is just strolling around with the ghosts of the Romans in this 2,000-year-old arena.

Finds from Polensium are displayed in the Archaeological Museum just south of the amphitheatre.

Other interesting remnants of Roman rule include the **Triumphal Arch of Sergius**, the **Temple of Augustus** and the remains of the **Roman Forum**. The tourist office offers maps detailing the most

The pretty town of Rovinj

worthwhile sights of Polensium, traces of which can be found in such inauspicious places as the bus station, where the Roman walls can be seen.

Pula's **Cathedral of St Mary** is a testament to the eventual victory of Christianity over paganism here. Parts date from the fourth century, and some of the building was erected from stone pilfered from the Roman amphitheatre after the demise of Polensium. The cathedral has undergone numerous renovations over the years, many of which can be easily traced, such as the fourth-century rear wall, the thirteenth-century sacristy and the seventeenth-century bell tower.

Vodnjan

The road north to the resorts passes through **Vodnjan**, 10km (6 miles) from Pula. This nondescript inland town is known for its 'mummies' in St Blaise's Church. Some devout Croats believe that the mummies possess magical powers, but many of today's visitors just come for the ghoulish appeal of viewing the desiccated corpses of St Nikolosa Bursa, St Giovanni Olini and St Leon Bembo. Vodnjan itself is worth a wander, and there are a few, small restaurants if you want to stop off for lunch or dinner.

Rovinj

About 50km (30 miles) north along the E751 from Pula is **Rovinj**, the most attractive, and along with Poreč, one of the most popular towns on the Istrian littoral. The approach to Rovinj is spectacular, with views of the old town clustered on a hilly peninsula in a collage of orange roof tiles and cobbled streets. In summer, the streets can be busy, but the big hotel developments and campsites are outside the old town so much of the historical core remains unspoilt.

Dominating Rovinj from its highest spot is the church of **St Euphemia**. This eighteenth-century Baroque creation features Istria's tallest bell tower, which has been used for centuries by local fishermen for weather forecasts and as a landmark for seeking their way home. Legend has it that the body of St Euphemia arrived shrouded in mystery in her weighty sarcophagus on the Rovinj shoreline. No one could budge the bulky stone tomb until a local boy and his two cows conspired with divine intervention to spirit her to her final resting place. The sarcophagus is now in the church.

The **Heritage Museum** (www.muzej-rovinj.hr/; charge) delves into the town's long history. In addition to preserving the cultural and artistic heritage of the region it plays host to a number of temporary exhibitions and has a permanent collection of Istrian folk costumes and finds from local archeological digs, as well as paintings from the fifteenth and sixteenth centuries.

Children will enjoy the **Rovinj Aquarium** (*Akvarij*; 52 804 712; charge) located outside of the old town. The aquarium was opened in 1891, and although it is not exactly state of the art, it is home to a colourful collection of Istrian marine life.

ISTRIAN WINES

Ancient Greek settlers first brought wine production to Dalmatia, while in Istria, wine has been popular since Roman times. Under the Communists, the focus was placed on quantity over quality, and then during the Croatian War of Independence in the early 1990s, many vineyards were destroyed. Since the 1990s, burgeoning boutique wineries and growing brands have brought Croatian wine back to the international market. Large-scale producers and small family-run vineyards have invested in modern machinery and techniques, improving the standards of what were already fine wines.

Look out for Muscatel and Malvazija whites and the Teran red. These wines are available in shops all over Istria, though they are expensive when bottled – which is why many locals travel out to vineyards themselves to buy in bulk. The Istria County Tourist Association has produced the Guide to the Wine Roads of Istria with a map and details of the vineyards where you can sample and buy wine. It is available from tourist offices in Istria.

Rovinj old town, Istria

One of Rovinj's most appealing streets is **Grisia**, a narrow lane that ascends north from sea level up to the church of St Euphemia. Grisia is charming enough in itself, with fine views of the church unfolding as you climb, but it is also home to Rovinj's thriving artistic community. The enlightened local authorities have encouraged painters and artisans to live and work along Grisia, and more than a dozen small shops now have the artists' eclectic work on sale. Much of it is geared towards the tourist trade, but there are some interesting pieces to be found if you look carefully. Simply walking through the open-air market is enjoyable regardless of whether you are in the market for artwork.

One of the great pleasures in Rovinj is doing nothing other than dipping in and out of the Adriatic Sea. As with many Istrian towns, there are no real beaches, only a ramble of rocks around the old town peninsula, as well as concrete platforms and steps for less agile bathers. Lining the waterfront on the southern side of the town are cafés and restaurants.

Poreč

About 30km (20 miles) north of Rovinj is **Poreč**, which along with Rovinj is the heart of Istria's tourist industry, and its attractive Venetian-style architecture. Despite throngs of holidaymakers, the old town retains its character as many of the area's hotels and campsites are located in the purpose-built resort of Zelena Laguna. In high season, Poreč's waterfront is lined with bobbing tour boats; the restaurants offer tourist menus and there are myriad watersports on offer.

Tourism apart, Poreč's greatest attraction is the UNESCO World Heritage listed **Basilica of Euphrasius** (www.zupaporec.com/euphrasian-basilica.html; free), one of the most remarkable examples of Byzantine art in the world. The scattering of buildings inside the main complex occupy the site of a fourth-century church, whose mosaics can be seen in the apse just inside the main door of today's basilica. The ebullient gold and mother-of-pearl studded scenes of the Virgin and Child, the Annunciation and Visitation are captivating.

The Romans made Poreč what it is today with their sturdy town plan, and its main thoroughfares are still evident, though these days they are lined with shops, cafés and restaurants. Follow Decumanus down from Zagrebačka to trace the heart of the Roman town, a walk culminating at the Forum. Look out for the **Romanesque House**, built many centuries after the Romans left Istria. It has managed to preserve its characteristic look despite numerous renovations. Visits are by appointment only.

Other coastal resorts

Between Rovinj and Poreč is **Vrsar**, a quieter resort than Poreč which sports a beautiful marina and old town.

To the north of Poreč towards the Slovenian border are the resorts of **Umag** and **Novigrad**. Novigrad is the more attractive of the two – a sort of mini-Rovinj complete with a bell tower overlooking a town that curls around a peninsula. Though there are some unattractive hotel developments dating from the communist era, there is a marina and some good fish restaurants. Umag is appealing in a different way and has its moment in the spotlight every July when the Croatian Tennis Open brings in big international names, as well as local stars.

On Istria's quieter east coast, hillside **Labin** is the largest and most interesting settlement. Its neighbour, **Rabac**, offers excellent beaches and lively nightlife.

Novigrad waterfront houses

Boat trips from the coastal resorts

Between May and October there are regular boat excursions from all the Istrian resorts. The trips often include lunch and can be booked at hotels or at the boats themselves on the previous evening, or even, subject to availability, on the day. One of the most popular excursions is to the **Brijuni Islands** (www.np-brijuni.hr/en), a string of verdant islands granted national park status in 1983. Public access is allowed on only two of them, Veli Brijun and Mali Brijun; even then visitors either have to be staying at one of the hotels on Veli Brijun or be on one of the organized tours.

The islands were once a retreat for Tito, who spent much of his time entertaining world dignitaries and film stars here. These guests brought many of the animals at Brijuni Safari Park as gifts for the communist leader.

Limski Zaljev (Lim Fjord) is one of the most dramatic day trips. The steep walls of the fjord are covered with lush vegetation, and were once a hideaway for pirates and the setting for Richard Widmark's 1963 Viking film, *The Long Ships*. Its waterside restaurants are an excellent place for lunch, particularly the Viking, which was named after the film and displays some of its memorabilia. Visitors with their own transport can also take the old road from Rovinj to Poreč and stop off to savour some of the best seafood in Croatia.

Istrian interior

While the coast attracts the holidaymakers, the hinterland remains mostly unexplored. The rolling green landscape of scenic hill towns and winding roads is blessed with many fine wines, truffles to match the best Italy and France have to offer, and rustic places to savour the food and drink of the region. This is where the *agroturizam* movement opened up traditional farmhouses as restaurants and guesthouses a couple of decades ago. (see page 123).

A 35km (22-mile) drive east of Poreč is Istria's rather unlikely regional capital, **Pazin**, which is a good base for exploring the interior, although it is by no means as attractive as many of the smaller hill towns. The main sights in the town are the castle, incorporating the Ethnographic Museum of Istria and the town museum (www.emi.hr; charge), and the plunging limestone gorge that descends more than 100m (328ft) below the town centre. This vertiginous drop was said to have been the inspiration for Jules Verne when he propelled the eponymous protagonist of his novel *Mathias Sandorf* over the abyss. Some say the spectacular chasm may also have prompted Dante to write his *Inferno*.

The archetypal Istrian hill town is **Motovun**, situated 20km (12 miles) northeast of Poreč, and well-known for its annual film festival that celebrates indie productions. Motovun has it all:

Pazin is perched on a limestone cliff

View over the Kvarner Gulf

vineyards on the approach through the valley of the Mirna River and the winding road up the green slopes to an orange-roofed old town that harbours Roman and Venetian remnants. There are cosy cafés and small restaurants to enjoy the local cuisine. The best way to get acquainted with Motovun is to take to its Venetian walls and wander around the old stone defences, surveying the tiled rooftops on one side and the rolling countryside on the other.

Buzet is also renowned for its high-quality truffles. Every November there is a truffle festival, and in season the men and their dogs can be seen heading out into the forests hunting for the pungent delicacy. Restaurants all over Istria serve truffles with pasta as well as steak with black truffle sauce. Those who are self-catering may like to buy truffle products at the Zigante Tartufi outlets in Grožnjan, Buzet, Livade, Tušilović and Buje.

Grožnjan, to the west of Motovun, is a shining example of what can be done with a crumbling old town by forward-thinking local authorities. Grožnjan was slowly dying until artists and artisans were tempted into its narrow, cobbled streets by the promise of free or low rents and refurbished houses. Today, the art scene flourishes with more than twenty art galleries and studios. An international summer college for young musicians is based in Grožnjan, which helps transform this hilly outcrop into an almost continuous stage with the sounds of classical music, jazz, and other sounds nearly everywhere. The town is pedestrianized, making it ideal for an unhurried morning or afternoon browsing through the workshops.

About 40km (25 miles) east of Grožnjan is **Hum**, which holds the Guinness World Record for being the world's smallest town – it has just one circular street and square accommodating the houses, post office, church and other essentials that qualify it as a town. Now that it has cottoned on to its place in the world, this charming settlement and its handful of residents are making the most of it.

Kvarner Gulf

Highlights

- **Rijeka**, see page 62
- **The Opatija Riviera**, see page 63
- **Paklenica National Park**, see page 65
- **Kvarner Gulf Islands**, see page 66

The Kvarner Gulf is the wide, island-studded basin that separates the Istrian peninsula in the north from Dalmatia in the south. In some ways it offers the best of both areas, with well-developed resort facilities and rustic towns to explore. Transport links are good, too: the motorway stretches from Zagreb to Rijeka (there's a toll to pay) and much of Dalmatia, and there are ferry services to Dalmatia and train links from Zagreb to Rijeka.

The most interesting areas of the Kvarner Gulf are the coastal towns and the islands, whereas much of the hinterland is unforgiving and undeveloped. The harsh face of the interior is omnipresent with the voluminous wall of the Velebit range hanging over the gulf and bringing in summer thunderstorms and the bitter *bura* wind. The Velebit mountains also give walkers and mountaineers spectacular views over the Kvarner Gulf.

Rijeka

Situated on the Kvarner Gulf's northern shore, **Rijeka** is the principal city in the region and an important transport hub, with a major ferry terminal and an airport on the nearby island of Krk. The town experienced a golden age as a thriving Adriatic port under the Habsburg Empire. From the nineteenth century, trains linked it to Vienna and Budapest. Today, this industrial metropolis is making a concerted effort to tempt tourists to stay for a day or two rather than breeze through in search of the next ferry or bus. Its harbour includes a number of restaurants, bars and cafés and the annual Rijeka Carnival, which takes place in January and February each year attracts huge crowds.

The seafront town of Volosko

Rijeka's main thoroughfare is the elegant Korzo, home to many of its best shops, cafés and most impressive buildings. To get a feel for the city, idle for a while at a café and survey the scene. Then venture into **Stari Grad** (old town) through the medieval City Tower and you will come upon another world, far removed from the nineteenth-century order outside. This scruffy historic quarter has a Roman arch, as well as the church of **St Vitus**, dedicated to the city's patron saint. Parts of the church date from the seventeenth century and were modelled on Santa Maria della Salute Basilica in Venice.

NOTES

Opatija has an air of faded grandeur. Enjoy a Sachertorte and a Viennese-style coffee in the Hotel Milenij's terrace café, which overlooks the sea, and truly capture the spirit of its nineteenth-century heyday.

For a sweeping view of the city, take a bus up the steep hill to the thirteenth-century castle at **Trsat**, or tackle the 561 steps. In the past, pilgrims would climb the steps on their knees. This may not be one of Europe's most attractive castles, but the views are good and in summer there are classical concerts in the grounds and a pleasant open-air café. Nearby, the church of **Our Lady of Trsat** is a place of pilgrimage, particularly for women whose messages of thanks and pleas for help line the interior. The Catholic Church holds that this was where the Holy House of Mary came to rest in the thirteenth century after fleeing Nazareth en route to Italy. It is said to have remained on the site where the church is today for three years before continuing its journey across the Adriatic to Loreto.

The Opatija Riviera

The eastern extremity of the Istrian peninsula, a short drive west of Rijeka, was a favourite playground for nineteenth-century Austrians, who came here to escape the winter cold and seek cures for their various ailments. With a famously mild climate afforded by its unparalleled setting between the Adriatic and the Učka Mountains, it is easy to see its attraction.

Opatija itself is one of the few year-round coastal resorts in Croatia, with an ever-increasing number of luxury hotels and good restaurants. The town has retained many of its grand nineteenth-century hotel buildings, as well as the Lungomare, a waterfront promenade that is packed with people in summer and is still a pleasant place for strolls even in winter. The graceful waterfront gardens and elegant buildings still speak of the affluent days when Opatija was one of Europe's top tourist destinations, not least following the completion of the rail line from Vienna to Trieste in 1873.

View over Baška on the island of Krk

HIKING OPPORTUNITIES

In addition to visiting Paklenica National Park, keen hikers may like to explore the rugged Mt Učka massif, accessible from towns along the coast between Poklon Pass in the north to Plomin Bay in the south. Facilities are not extensive, but there are a few mountain lodges and stone cottages for hikers, a restaurant at Poklon and a viewpoint tower on the peak of Vojak. For Vojak, the highest peak (1,396 metres/4,580ft), climb through Lovran's old town and follow the steps that lead up the hillside to the village of Liganj and on to the hamlets of Didici and Ivulici. The ascent can be managed in around four hours but take provisions.

The Lungomare connects Opatija with **Volosko** to the north and **Lovran** to the south. Sleepy Volosko makes for an enjoyable morning stroll, particularly if you reward your efforts with lunch in one of its seafood restaurants. Lovran is a mini-Opatija with some hotels and buildings that hark back to the riviera's golden age. There are good cafés and restaurants and opportunities for bathing. Lovran is also a good base if you are planning to walk in the **Učka mountains**; information is available from the local tourist office.

Paklenica National Park

The scenery southeast of Rijeka is spectacular, with the Velebit mountain range towering above the barren coast, but there are few attractions other than the small town of **Senj**. In the sixteenth century, Senj became infamous as the base from which the Uskok warriors would set forth to attack shipping on the Adriatic.

Further south, the **Paklenica National Park** ❼ (https://np-paklenica.hr) is a paradise for walkers, mountaineers and rock climbers. UNESCO-listed since 2017, the park is well organized and information and maps are obtainable from the national park office in Stari Grad, which is where most spend the night. From the town of Stari Grad a series of trails caters for all levels of agility and ability. If you are planning a long hike, basic mountain hut-style accommodation is available, but hotels (and hunting) are banned in the park. There are two main gorges: Mala Paklenica and Velika Paklenica, literally 'small' and 'big' Paklenica. The latter is the more user-friendly, with a well-marked main trail that snakes up in a two-hour walk from the car park. Climbers can start with the sheer rock face that greets visitors at the entrance to the park.

Kvarner Gulf Islands

Krk ❽ is a popular island, particularly among central Europeans, for whom it is an easy drive south and across the bridge that links it to the mainland. **Krk Town** retains a semblance of its historic ambience with a solid old core and a few worthwhile churches. The nearby resort of **Baška** is the most appealing on the island, with 2km (1.2 mile) of Blue Flag beach and the brooding Velebit mountains visible on the mainland. As well as having modern hotels and campsites, Baška has a small old quarter with good seafood restaurants and pension-style accommodation. It is essential to book ahead in high season as foreign and Croatian visitors descend on the area.

Rab's lovely old town

Baška is famous for the twelfth-century Baška Tablet (now in the Academy of Arts and Science in Zagreb), the oldest existing example of Glagolitic script, the precursor of Cyrillic and used in Croatia until well into the Middle Ages.

Wine-lovers should head to the northeastern coastal town of Vrbnik. Set among high cliffs, this attractive town is home to some of Croatia's best white wines, namely vrbinčka žlahtina. Try it in one of the town's many wine cellars and restaurants.

A small car ferry departs daily in summer from Baška across the channel to the island of **Rab**, home to beautiful **Rab Town**. It is also possible to take a ferry from Jablanac in Northern Dalmatia across to Rab, which is worth considering if you are planning a journey along the coastline.

The island has a number of modest resorts and villages, but Rab Town is its undoubted star, with a well-preserved old quarter punctuated by church spires and cobbled streets. Swimming in the shadow of the pine trees beneath the old walls is a memorable experience. There are also regular taxi-boats serving beaches located in isolated bays around the island. The village of Lopar has one of the best sandy beaches in northern Croatia, its shallow waters ideal for families with small children.

Rab Town's nightlife is amongst the liveliest on the Kvarner Gulf, making it popular with younger travellers. But it is also popular with families and the island has an unmistakable buzz in high season.

Although you can see **Pag** from Rab, and there is a catamaran service to Novalja on Pag, getting there can often be frustrating. For those staying in Rab Town, the island is best reached on an organized boat trip. Pag is famous for its lamb, sheep's milk cheese (*paški sir*), found on menus throughout Croatia, and also for intricate hand-made lace. **Novalja** has a reputation for being one of Croatia's party towns, with a cluster of noisy nightclubs around the beach. Some are open 24/7 during the summer. More tranquil **Pag Town** is the best base for exploring the island.

St Donat's Church

Of the two main islands on the western side of the Kvarner Gulf – Cres and Lošinj – Cres (pronounced *tsres*) is the most northerly, with ferry connections from Istria, Rijeka and Krk. **Cres Town** makes a good base for travelling the length of the island. Colourful houses encircle its busy harbour from where fishermen supply the local restaurants.

Lošinj lies across a narrow channel to the south of Cres. The two main towns are Mali and Veli Lošinj. **Mali Lošinj** attracts those in search of louder bars and a choice of day trips. In contrast, **Veli Lošinj** has a more rustic appeal, but enough facilities to ensure an enjoyable stay. There are a number of islets dotted around Lošinj that can be explored by day, and by night Italian influenced seafood awaits at the waterfront restaurants of both towns.

Dalmatia

Highlights

- **Northern Dalmatia**, see page 70
- **Southern Dalmatia: Split**, see page 76
- **South of Split**, see page 78
- **Dubrovnik**, see page 79
- **Dalmatian Islands**, see page 84

Dalmatia ❾ is the long sinewy arm of Croatia that sweeps south-east from the Kvarner Gulf towards the border with Montenegro, hugging the Bosnian border for much of its length. Its coastline is punctuated by historic cities and towns and littered with myriad offshore islands, each with its own allure. The Homeland War hit parts of Dalmatia badly, and while the images of Dubrovnik being shelled made TV news bulletins around the world (see page 30), it was the northern cities of Zadar and Šibenik that fared the worst.

Today there are few obvious signs of war damage and you can spend a week or two in Dalmatia without noticing anything unusual. Compared to Istria, much of Dalmatia's tourist industry is a bit lower key – with the major exception of Dubrovnik and islands such as Hvar, which now suffer from a touch of overtourism. There is plenty to see in a region where the constants are outstanding scenery, rich layers of history and the omnipresent waters of the Adriatic.

DOLPHINS OF LOŠINJ

The dolphins of Lošinj attracted international attention with the launch of the award-winning Adriatic Dolphin Project in 1987. Covering the islands of Cres and Lošinj, the project aims to discover more about the dolphins' way of life, as well as to help in their protection. The crystal waters and rugged coastline are a haven for these delightful mammals, something that yachtsmen can confirm, with many passing boats enjoying a very special escort.

Swimming with dolphins is prohibited, but those wanting to get involved can volunteer to take part in the project. When the weather is suitable the time is spent out at sea recording, dating and tracking the animals, and direct contact with them is common. In poor weather, there are lectures and the chance to delve into the project's archives. For details see www.blue-world.org, where you can also 'adopt a dolphin'.

Northern Dalmatia

During the Homeland War, **Zadar** ⑩ was cut off from the rest of the country as Serb forces pummelled the historic centre. Today the city is firmly back on its feet, with museums of interest, a revamped waterfront, hotels and lively nightlife.

Zadar's old town is spectacularly situated on a peninsula, its sturdy walls and hefty gates once protecting it from attack. **Široka Ulica**, the arrow-straight Roman road that dissects the old town, passes many of the key sights as it makes its way west to the Adriatic. The post-World War II buildings that replaced those destroyed by Allied bombs are all too evident, but amid them is the Baroque church of **St Simeon**. Its treasure is the Romanesque sarcophagus by the Milanese goldsmith Francesco di Antonio da Sesto, embellished with reliefs depicting the life of the saint and the rescue of his relics from the Venetians by Louis I.

Further west is **Narodni Trg**, the square that took over from the Roman Forum as the hub of city life during the Middle Ages. Fronting the square is a Venetian-era **Town Loggia** (loža; charge), housing an art gallery and temporary exhibitions. Also on the square is the sixteenth-century Guard House with its high clock tower, as well as a couple of pavement cafés. From Narodni Trg you can head north through the old Sea Gate and across a footbridge to the newer part of the city.

A 10-minute walk west along Široka Ulica from Narodni Trg brings you to the site of the Roman Forum. Here, among the stony remains of what was once Zadar's focal point, stands the city's symbol, **St Donat's Church**. The cylindrical church was built in the ninth century using, in part, stones culled from the Roman Forum, which can be recognized by their Latin inscriptions. The compact two-storey interior, with its tightly packed stone walls, is unlike that of any other religious building in Croatia. Today it no longer functions as a place of worship, but in summer its fine acoustics can be appreciated when it is used as a venue for classical and

Šibenik Cathedral

folk music concerts. These include the Donat Festival held every July and August, which has been running for well over sixty years.

Facing St Donat's Church across the Forum is the worthwhile **Archaeological Museum** (Arheološki muzej; http://amzd.hr; charge). On display are finds from excavations all over northern Dalmatia, with the Roman era in Zadar obviously well represented.

Zadar Cathedral, on the northwestern side of the Forum, dates from the twelfth century, although much on view today was painstakingly reconstructed after Allied bombing during World War II. The slightly incongruous-looking bell tower was a nineteenth-century addition to the Romanesque cathedral.

The **Zadar Museum of Antique Glass** (Muzej antičkog stakla; www.mas-zadar.hr/en; charge), in the refurbished nineteenth-century Cosmacendi Palace, contains one of the best ancient glassware collections outside Italy. Zadar's art installations on the Riva promenade have also attracted international acclaim and have become the town's main tourist attractions. The *Sea Organ* consists of a series of stone steps leading into the sea, with underwater pipes creating eerie sound effects – many sit here for ours listening to the sea sing. The *Greeting to the Sun* is 22m in diameter and creates an intricate light show on the surface of the promenade at sunset. It charges during the day via solar under the glass.

Zadar's beaches are north and south of the old town, with many rocky stretches among some gravel and sand. Borik and Diklo are north of the town, and Kolovare to the south is one of the most popular, combining sand and gravel. You'll find plenty of facilities for children including play areas.

About an hour's drive south of Zadar along the motorway or E65 is the city of **Šibenik**. Until the 1990s, it was a major industrial centre, but the war put paid to the traditional enterprises and the city became one of the poorest in the country. Atypically for the Croatian coastline, there are no traces of Roman civilization here as the Croatian kings established the city a millennium ago. Hence the jumbled streets of the old town and the low-rise muddle of houses, which are in contrast to the elegant order of Roman Poreč or Zadar. Nevertheless, the shape of its coastline made it a natural home for Croatia's state-of-the-art marina for superyachts, D-Marin Mandalina. This 5-Anchor-rated millionaires' playground is also an official port of entry into Republic of Croatia.

The city's main attraction, dominating the city and skyline, is **Šibenik Cathedral** (free), a UNESCO World Heritage Site. Much of the cathedral was the work of Zadar-born Juraj Dalmatinac (c.1400–73), though it took over a century to build and has many different influences incorporated into its grand design, from late Gothic to Renaissance. Also in the city centre is the restored medieval **garden of St Lawrence's Monastery** (free).

Skradinski Buk falls, Krka National Park

Just outside Šibenik, in the village of Dubrava, is Croatia's only **Falconry Centre**, where you can learn about the ancient art and the conservation of birds of prey. Half an hour's drive from Šibenik in the village of Pakovo Selo is **Etnoland** (https://etnoland.com; charge), a well-designed discovery park revealing the secrets of Dalmatian life before the age of electricity.

Around Zadar and Šibenik, the main resort areas of **Borik**, **Biograd**, **Solaris** and **Vodice** all have extensive resort facilities, and a range of hotels, restaurants and nightlife.

An hour's drive south along the motorway or E65 past the pretty resort of Primošten is **Trogir**, which also features on UNESCO's World Heritage list, and justifiably so. Trogir's old quarter is a beautifully preserved medieval oasis set on its own islet. In high season, holidaymakers throng the old streets of fourteenth- and fifteenth-century buildings, relaxing in the seafood restaurants and watching the luxury yachts come and go from the cafés along the Riva promenade.

Trogir's most impressive attraction is its **cathedral** (charge for bell tower). The remarkable thirteenth-century west portal is the work of Croatian sculptor Master Radovan and depicts scenes from the life of Christ as well as images of local Dalmatian life. Inside is the superb Renaissance Chapel of St John, created by Nikola Firentinac, with its 160 sculpted heads of angels, cherubs and saints. In and around the cathedral square you can also admire the **Čipiko Palace**, **town hall**, **loggia** and **clock tower** and, nearby, the crumbling remains of **Kamerlengo Castle**, now used as an open-air cinema and events stage. You can walk up the stairs and admire the spectacular views.

Split's old town

Connected to Trogir by bridge is the small island of Čiovo, lined with pebbly beaches around the villages of Arbanije, Slatine. Scuba-divers are catered for along the beaches at Okrug Donji and Okrug Gornji. To visit one of the few sandy beaches in the region, take a boat ride from Trogir to the tiny island of Drvenik Mali.

An easy day trip inland from Zadar, Šibenik or Trogir is **Krka National Park** ⓫ (www.npkrka.hr; charge includes boat ride from Skradin to Skradinski Buk).

This natural wonderland of gorges and waterfalls on the River Krka may be lesser known than the Plitvice Lakes further north, but it is every bit as appealing and not usually as busy. From the village of **Skradin**, 16km (10 miles) from Šibenik, regular boats leave for the impressive **Skradinski Buk** and its seventeen separate falls. From Skradinski Buk additional cruises venture deeper into the park (additional fee). **Visovac**, with its Franciscan monastery set in the midst of Visovačko Lake, is alone worth the trip. Housed in the monastery's library is an ornately illustrated copy of *Aesop's Fables*, thought to be one of only three of its kind in the world. Some cruises continue on to **Roški Slap**, another waterfall.

Another highlight of the region is the **Kornati Islands National Park** (www.np-kornati.hr/en). George Bernard Shaw eulogized dreamily at the beauty of the 147 barren, inhospitable and waterless strips of rugged rock that make up the archipelago.

Kornat, which stretches some 25km (15 miles) in length and 2.5km (1.55 miles) in width, is the largest; others are little more than rugged rocks, their stark terrain shining like beacons against the blue of the Adriatic. The national park is accessible on day trips from many northern Dalmatian towns and resorts, particularly Murter. But undoubtedly the best way to savour the archipelago is to spend a week sailing in their challenging waters, stopping off at rustic restaurants and secluded bays.

From Šibenik there are some wonderfully undiscovered islands a quick ferry or boat trip away. **Prvić** and **Krapanj** each have boutique hotels and, together with **Zlarin** and the smaller surrounding islands, are popular for swimming holidays as the islands are close to each other and low lying.

The Zadar archipelago has some three hundred islands, the largest of which is Dugi otok. Its rocky coastline hides secluded coves and picturesque fishing ports, with its southeastern tip taken over by the Telašćica nature park (https://pp-telascica.hr) and its numerous islets and exquisite bays.

Southern Dalmatia: Split

Dalmatia's largest city, **Split** ⓬, was founded by the Roman emperor Diocletian in AD 295. His retirement palace, the remarkably intact complex of **Diocletian's Palace** Ⓐ – a UNESCO World Heritage Site – still forms the core of the city. Many of the original palace buildings have long since gone, although remnants of the basement rooms can be seen. Today, cafés, bars, shops, hotels and apartments jostle for space within the palace's protective outer walls, which enclose the old town.

In the palace complex is the octagonal **Cathedral of St Domnius** (Sv Duje Katedrala), which was originally built as Diocletian's mausoleum but later converted into a church. A black granite Egyptian sphinx can be seen to the right of the doorway. The cathedral's wooden doors were carved in 1214 by Andrija Buvina, a local sculptor, and depict scenes from the life of Christ. You can climb the Romanesque bell tower for bird's-eye views.

The cathedral overlooks the **Peristyle**, a colonnaded sunken square housing a café and restaurant that offers an atmospheric setting for refreshment.

North of Diocletian's Palace, through the **Golden Gate** (Zlatna Vrata), which originally led to the Roman town of Salona (see page 77), is the monumental sculpture of the tenth-century bishop Grgur of Nin (Gregory of Nin) by Ivan Meštrović (1929). Tradition claims that if you touch the statue's toe, a wish will be granted – the said toe is now a golden colour, polished over the years by the hands of passers-by. Opposite the statue is the purpose-built, high-tech **Split Gallery of Fine Arts** Ⓑ (www.galum.hr; charge) housing an surprisingly extensive selection of masterpieces.

For an insight into the life and work of the Split-born sculptor, the **Meštrović Gallery** (Galerija Meštrovića; 46 Šetalište Ivana Meštrovića; https://mestrovic.hr; charge), situated beneath the Marjan peninsula to the west of the town, features some of his most important work. It is housed in what was the sculptor's summer home.

Diocletian's Palace cathedral bell tower

Split is known for its vibrant nightlife, which centres on Diocletian's Palace until 10pm, after which, in summer, the bars and clubs that line the waterfront to the south become the focal point. Earlier in the evening, locals of all ages like to promenade along **Marmontova**, stopping off at one of the many open-air cafés that line the Riva.

A short walk away from the centre and the ferry terminal is the **Bačvice** complex, around Split's gently sloping sandy beach. Here, and in nearby **Zenta**, are a clutch of good restaurants and cafés looking out to sea.

About 5km (3 miles) inland from Split and accessible by local bus are the ruins of the once thriving Roman town of **Salona**. As the attacks of the Slavs in the seventh century took their toll on Salona, the citizens fled to Diocletian's Palace, thus ensuring its survival and the life that today still bustles within its stone walls. Remains dot the landscape of Salona, such as the amphitheatre that in its heyday played host to a baying 18,000-strong crowd. Continuing about 6km northeast, you will find the **Fortress of Klis**, a strategic point that saw numerous battles, but in modern times has gained fame as the city of Meereen from *Game of Thrones*.

A few miles north of Split are the sleepy villages of **Kaštela**, named after the fortifications that dominate each of the seven villages. Recent years have seen many foreigners purchase and then renovate the stone houses specifically for their old-world charms and magnificent views across Kaštela bay.

South of Split

South of Split is **Omiš**, the centre of Dalmatia's pirate history and its folk music (klapa), where an annual folk festival is held each summer. The scenery here is stunning and dramatic. The Biokovo Mountains appear to spring directly from the old town itself as they rise steeply around the Cetina river gorge, making the area popular with hikers, mountaineers and river rafters. Further along, tumbling down the hillside from the road towards the pine-fringed Adriatic beaches are

Dubrovnik is a remarkably picturesque city

the various resorts and towns of the **Makarska Riviera**. Offshore the Dalmatian islands of Brač and Hvar laze in the Adriatic sun. Such glorious scenery makes up for the occasional bland town, ugly development and the numerous campsites along this stretch of coast.

The most attractive of the smaller resorts is **Brela**, at the northern end of the Riviera. **Makarska** itself is a big, brash place with good shingle beaches nearby and a vibrant nightlife. Resorts to the south include **Tučepi**, **Podgora**, **Drvenik** and **Zaostrog**.

South of Makarska the new bridge delivers you straight to the **Pelješac Peninsula** without the need to pass through a tiny piece of coastal Bosnia as had been the case for twenty years. This unspoilt spit of land juts out into the Adriatic Sea and provides some of the best wines in Croatia, such as *Dingač* and *Postup*, as well as first-rate seafood. **Ston** is linked to Mali Ston by fourteenth-century fortifications, about half of which still remain, built to protect the saltpans from mainland marauders. It is well worth breaking the journey here or making a special trip from Dubrovnik to absorb the history and savour the oysters and mussels that are farmed in front of the restaurants.

Dubrovnik

The jewel in the crown of the Croatian tourism industry, **Dubrovnik** ⓭ is a walled city with immense visual appeal. Its historical and architectural significance was recognized by UNESCO as early as 1979, adding it to its list of World Heritage sites. During the Homeland War, the city was under siege for six months and tourist ground to a halt. Now, however, the city has the opposite problem – too many visitors, many of whom are on day-trips from the resorts or on cruises. It is the only place in Croatia afflicted by overtourism, though there are still quiet times when you can almost have the place to yourself. At the end of the 2010s, a new type of tourism specifically focused on *Game of Thrones* filming locations, only exacerbated this feeling of congestion in the summer months. The '*Thrones* Effect' has outlasted the TV show's end, and in summer the old town is so congested that those turning up without somewhere to stay will almost certainly be disappointed.

The city's history has been shaped by its perpetual struggle to retain its independence. Settlement in the area first took root in the seventh century when Dubrovnik was an island cut off from the mainland by a small channel. Its original name of Ragusa translates as 'rock', and the former moniker still appears on flags and museums in the city. Even today, its citizens are proud that Dubrovnik's sturdy fortifications have never been breached, though in truth the city owed its freedom more to the skill of its diplomats than to its military strength. For centuries it was a major trading centre, with ships flitting all over the Mediterranean and beyond; by the fifteenth century, its boundaries extended as far as Ston to the north and to Cavtat in the south.

In 1667, a massive earthquake ripped through the region. The damage to Dubrovnik was devastating, with the old core of the city, including its fine Renaissance buildings, practically levelled and more than five thousand people killed. The rebuilding programme was fortunately carefully managed, resulting in the fine baroque centre that we see today. But the city never really regained its former strength as a trading power and at the beginning of the nineteenth century came under the influence of Napoleonic France. It declined into a sleepy backwater until the twentieth century, when tourists first started taking an interest. Today, its tourist industry is as slick and good at making money as its merchants were in the sixteenth century.

To get a real feel for Dubrovnik, you need to take to the **medieval walls** (www.wallsofdubrovnik.com; charge), that encircle the old town, opening up vignettes of local life and providing a bird's-eye view of all of the main attractions. The climb is quite steep in parts as the sturdy walls rise up the hillside from the **Pile Gate** Ⓐ, the main entrance to the city, before running along a ridge and descending past the **Ploče Gate**. The southern walls plunge towards the Adriatic and make for great photos at sunset.

Inside Dubrovnik's city walls

Stradun Ⓑ, also known as Placa, is the polished artery that runs through the heart of Dubrovnik, with sights to the left and right and a sprinkling of pleasant pavement cafés. Prijeko, the narrow street running parallel to Stradun, becomes an almost continuous line of restaurants in season, their tables packed with diners.

At the western extremity of Stradun is the **Great Fountain of Onofrio**, the culmination of a system that has brought fresh water to the city since 1444. The circular domed well, with its sixteen water-spouting stone heads, is named after its designer Onofrio della Cava, an Italian who worked in the Dubrovnik region. According to some, it is lucky to drink at the well, but it was originally intended merely for washing on entering the city. A more minor

Dubrovnik viewed from above

fountain, known as the **Small Fountain of Onofrio**, is located near the church of St Blaise (see page 82).

To the east, Stradun leads to **Luža Square**, site of a cluster of historic buildings. The sixteenth-century **Sponza Palace** Ⓒ served as a bank, customs house, mint and treasury, before its current role as home to the state archives. This remarkable collection records the history and administration of Ragusa from the thirteenth century until its fall at the beginning of the nineteenth century. A shop selling facsimiles of historical documents is found in the palace's courtyard, as is the Memorial Room to the Defenders of Dubrovnik, with portraits of those who died during the 1991–2 siege. The courtyard is an atmospheric venue for musical performances during the Dubrovnik Summer Festival held every July and August.

At the southern end of Luža Square stands **Orlando's Column** (also known as Roland's Column) dating from 1418. It commemorates a mysterious figure who is said to have helped fight off Saracen pirates in the eighth century and, in doing so, earned the city's eternal gratitude. Orlando continues to play his part in Dubrovnik life as his column is where the start of the Dubrovnik Festival is declared every year.

Opposite is the eighteenth-century church of **St Blaise** (Crkva Sv Vlaho; free), named after the patron saint of Dubrovnik. Above the high altar stands a silver figure of St Blaise holding a scale model of the city: look out for similar representations of the saint elsewhere in the city.

A short walk from the church is the **Rector's Palace** Ⓓ (Knežev Dvor). This palatial building is a fitting residence for a figure who, in theory at least, was the most powerful person in the city. However, the honour of being rector was modified slightly by the fact that his family was not allowed to live with him and he was forbidden from leaving the palace unless on official business.

Constructed in the mid-fifteenth century, the palace was the seat of the Ragusan government as well as housing a lethal gunpowder store that ignited with devastating effect on a couple of occasions. The present building dates mainly from 1739 and is in Baroque style with a few Gothic details. On the ground floor of the palace are prison cells and on the upper floor are the state apartments and the former courtroom and judicial chambers. The palace's atrium makes a lovely concert venue.

Nearby is the **cathedral** (charge for treasury), which was almost totally destroyed by the earthquake of 1667. The interior comes alive with dramatic celebrations of Mass and classical concerts during the Dubrovnik Festival. Note the compelling *Assumption* by Titian on the main altar. The adjoining treasury displays a horde of gold reliquaries, including the Byzantine skull case of St Blaise. A local legend tells of how Richard the Lionheart was saved from a shipwreck while returning from the Crusades and by way of thanks funded the building of the first cathedral.

In a narrow side street between the Stradun and Prijeko, near Pile Gate, **War Photo Limited** (www.warphotoltd.com; charge) is an intriguing gallery devoted to photojournalism from war zones around the world. Ukraine, Yemen and Gaza feature heavily in current exhibitions.

Most of Dubrovnik's other sites are in the very compact area inside the city walls, mostly off Stradun or Luža Square. They include the Franciscan and Dominican monasteries, the Maritime Museum, the Rupe Granary (housing the Ethnographic Museum), the Jesuit Church and the city's synagogue. Outside the town, the **Homeland War Museum** (www.mdrd.hr; charge) on the site of the Imperial Fort at the top of Srđ mountain is worth a visit even just for the view itself. The Dubrovnik Cable Car (www.dubrovnikcablecar.com) is an easy, if someway pricey, way to reach the summit.

The city is at its liveliest during the **Dubrovnik Festival** (www.dubrovnik-festival.hr), held mid-July to mid-August. This arts extravaganza features theatre, opera and musical performances, and many historical buildings are used as venues.

Those with a few days in Dubrovnik may want to make a refreshing trip over to the beaches of the 'cursed' wooded island of **Lokrum**, just offshore. Boats run regularly to the island despite the curse, but visitors are not allowed to stay overnight. **Cavtat**, on the mainland near the airport, is a popular and quieter holiday destination, with an attractive waterfront lined with cafés and restaurants. It makes a great base for diving and attracts luxury yachts. The village juts out on the edge of a peninsula, where boats from Dubrovnik regularly arrive. Buses to Cavtat are a less scenic – and less expensive – option.

Dalmatian Islands

The city of Split is a good base for exploring the Dalmatian Islands. Most people head straight for the island beaches, but don't ignore the settlements and rustic restaurants inland where island life started, away from marauding pirates.

Just half an hour across the water is **Brač**, Croatia's third largest island, featuring Bol's **Žlatni Rat** (Golden Cape), the country's best-known shingle/sand beach. This cuts scenically into the Adriatic like a shark's fin, attracting countless sun-worshippers and windsurfers. **Bol** itself has a pleasant old town and is a centre for walks in the surrounding hills. A longer walk, or a short drive by car and a reasonably challenging hour's walk from the car park, takes you to the time capsule of **Hermitage Blaca**. Originally a cave shelter for two monks who arrived from the mainland in 1551, it became a flourishing monastery until the last monk, an acclaimed

Hvar's main square

NOTES

Tito set up base in a cave on Vis during World War II. From here, he conducted many military operations and hosted Churchill's envoy.

astronomer, died in 1963. Strikingly cut into the rocks, the buildings and other historic treasures have been preserved as a museum.

The neighbouring island of **Hvar** ⓮ is a favourite with international celebrities and has become one of Croatia's most visited destinations. **Hvar Town** attracts most of the attention as well-heeled travellers throng its cafés, restaurants and growing number of expensive nightclubs. They pile into the Riva that leads around the busy little harbour to the sixteenth-century St Stephen's Cathedral that dominates the main square. As its popularity grows, so do its prices, which are markedly higher in Hvar Town than in other parts of the Adriatic. The unassuming town of Stari Grad, added to UNESCO's World Heritage list for its old town and plain, is the place to enjoy the island's slower pace and less showy cultural life. In this sunniest of Croatia's islands, lavender is one of its biggest industries, with most of the production coming from small family-owned plots. The island even hosts an annual Lavender Festival each June in a little village just outside of Hvar Town.

Just off Brač's west coast lies the smaller and almost completely undiscovered island of **Šolta**, a mass of olive groves and vineyards with a handful of sleepy settlements. The most notable is west-facing Maslinica, with its beautiful sunsets and upmarket hotel and restaurant in the restored eighteenth-century Baroque castle.

Vis is the furthest island from the Croatian mainland and is quite unlike any of the others. First populated by the Greeks in the fourth century BC many of Europe's major powers fought over it down through the centuries including Austria, Italy, Germany and Britain, the latter two during World War II. Tourism was restricted here until 1989, as the island was used as a Yugoslav naval base. As a result,

Historic stone steps in the ancient town of Vis

its population density is low compared with other parts of Croatia. Despite its diminutive size, the island is renowned for its wine production, with tastings offered in family-run cellars.

Vis Town curves around a bay with its most appealing quarter, Kut, where wealthy Venetians built their homes during the sixteenth century. The Franciscan monastery features gravestones by the celebrated Croatian sculptor Ivan Rendić (1849–1932), as well as a mass grave for Austrian sailors killed in a sea battle off Vis in 1866.

Across the mountains from Vis Town is the fishing village of **Komiža**. As you approach, the church of St Nicholas, on a vine-covered bluff, offers a shady respite from the summer heat; its nearby cemetery contains the ornate tombs of notable local families. In Komiža itself there is a modest **Maritime Museum** that testifies to the town's fruitful association with the Adriatic. From Komiža you can take a boat trip in summer to the islet of **Biševo**, where, between 11am–noon depending on the season, the Blue Grotto (Modra špilja) is illuminated by a brilliant blue light, similar to the celebrated Blue Cave off Capri.

Further along the coastline, the island of **Korčula** ⓯ perches on the western end of the western end of the Pelješac Peninsula (see page 79). **Korčula Town** is one of the most attractive settlements on the coastline, jutting out from the mountains on its own peninsula. It can be visited on a lengthy day trip from Dubrovnik, but is also an excellent place to spend a few days. Surrounded by solid medieval walls, the old town is laid out on a tight grid system.

Vis monastery

The locals claim that the legendary explorer Marco Polo hails from the town, and you can visit the **Marco Polo House** (www.gradskimuzej-korcula.hr; charge) where the explorer is said to have been born. **St Mark's Cathedral** combines Gothic and Renaissance styles and contains two paintings by Tintoretto, who spent time in Korčula as a student.

The island is dotted with several very good beaches, including the sandy beach about a fifteen-minute walk from Korčula Town at Luka Korčulanska. To the south are several beaches near Lumbarda and towards the west at the village of Blato.

Korčula is the birthplace of Croatia's traditional sword dance, the *moreška*, and performances are held in the small outdoor theatre in Korčula Town (ask at the tourist office for exact times and days).

South towards Dubrovnik, the island of **Mljet** is often overlooked, but not by Croatians who are very aware of its green and lush beauty. The **Mljet National Park**, (www.np-mljet.hr) centres upon two beautiful lakes, Malo Jezero (small lake) and Veliko Jezero (big lake), which are excellent for swimming, with crystal clear water and the shade of evergreen forests on the water's edge. There is a cycle trail around one of the lakes and it is possible to go on a boat trip out to **St Mary's Island** to visit its **monastery**, an atmospheric spot with a restaurant and café.

Nearer to Dubrovnik are the **Elafiti Islands**, a cluster of quiet settlements surrounded by evergreen vegetation and popular beaches. **Koločep** is the nearest to Dubrovnik and the smallest of the three inhabited islands, with two tiny villages, peaceful olive groves to wander past and a compact beach. **Lopud** is the most developed for tourists, with its lovely (and sandy) Sunj Beach on which to relax. **Šipan** is the largest, its grand palaces a reminder of when Dubrovnik nobles used the island as their summer retreat. All three islands get very busy in the summer with day-trippers from Dubrovnik, but time your visit right for a delicious lunch of fresh seafood.

Rafting on the Cetina River

Things to do

There is no shortage of activities on offer in Croatia. If you're looking for something adventurous, the Adriatic coast is a paradise for scuba diving, sailing and other watersports. Inland you can go rafting and canoeing on the rivers or hiking and climbing in the mountains. There are beaches to relax on, islands to discover and historic walled cities to explore. Festivals give insights into local arts and culture; shopping, entertainment and nightlife are all to be enjoyed.

Outdoor activities

Diving

Croatia is one of Europe's top scuba-diving destinations. There are dive centres all the way along the Croatian coastline from **Umag** and **Rovinj** in Istria to **Dubrovnik** and **Cavtat** in southern Dalmatia. The highlight for many is **Vis**, which has several diveable shipwrecks just off its coast and the **Blue Grotto** at Biševo (see page 88).

Other favourite destinations for divers are the **Kornati Islands**, **Mezanj Island** near Dugi Otok, **Rovinj** and, to the south, the shipwreck of the *Totonno*, which was lost off the Dalmatian coast near Dubrovnik during World War II.

Scuba diving is strictly regulated in Croatia and no one is allowed to dive without first obtaining a diving permit. To dive independently (OWD course), as opposed to with a registered diving centre, requires further permission. For more information contact the Croatian Tourist Board (www.croatia.hr).

Sailing

Croatia has become something of a paradise for yachting enthusiasts, with many choosing yacht hire for their summer holidays. There's a vast choice of boats, sailing schools and small cruise boats to choose from.

The Adriatic coast offers superb diving opportunities

The **islands around Split** offer short distances and plenty of shelter to those learning the ropes, whilst the **Kornati Islands** provide challenging navigation but beautiful scenery. Experienced sailors enjoy the winds around **Pelješac**, though everyone pays attention when the *bura* wind starts to blow.

There are over sixty marinas along the coast from Umag in the north of Istria to Cavtat in the very south of the country. Adriatic Croatia International is the biggest operator with 22 marinas. Some of the larger marinas are almost resorts in themselves, while others, such as those at Trogir and Rab, bring you right into the heart of the town.

Would-be sailors have the choice of going 'bareboat' by just chartering a boat themselves, or taking a skipper. For bareboat you will need at least one member of your party to be a qualified skipper who can use a VHF radio. If you choose the skippered option, the cost goes up and you have to take one less person along in your party as the hired skipper will also sleep aboard. The toughest parts of sailing, such as navigation, will be taken out of your hands, though you and other members of your party will be required to help out with the ropes.

The website of the Croatian National Tourist Office – www.croatia.hr – has a comprehensive section on sailing called 'Nautical'.

Other watersports

All the coastal resorts offer watersports, especially in Istria where larger hotels lay on everything from **waterskiing** to **parasailing**. Or you can simply go **snorkelling** in the crystal-clear Adriatic. Inland, the rivers Kupa and Cetina are suitable for both **rafting and canoeing**. Organized rafting trips set off regularly in season, subject to conditions.

Football

The most popular spectator sport in Croatia is undoubtedly football. Only seven years after declaring independence, Croatia achieved third place in the 1998 World Cup and in 2018 even reached the final. The Croatian national team play most of their games at the Maksimir Stadium in Zagreb, but also sometimes travel to Split and Varaždin. **Dinamo Zagreb** also play at Maksimir, regularly doing well in their domestic league and almost annually playing

NOTES

White-water rafting is possible on several of Croatia's rivers. The Kupa River, near Karlovac, offers some of the best rafting in Central Croatia. Towards the Adriatic, in the Gorski Kotar, rafting can be arranged on the Dobra River. From the Dalmatian coast it is easy to get to the Cetina River, where rafting can be enjoyed in spring and summer.

in the UEFA Champions League. Their great rivals have always been **Hajduk Split** from the southern city and big games between the two can be turbulent affairs. The most famous Croatian player to have succeeded on the international stage is Luka Modrić, formerly of Tottenham Hotspur and Real Madrid, now of AC Milan.

Tennis

The other major spectator sport in Croatia is tennis, with key players such as Ivan Dodig and Marin Čilić drawing big crowds for their matches. Mate Pavić and Nikola Mektić excel in men's doubles – in 2021, they won Wimbledon and the gold medal at the Olympics in Tokyo, becoming the first Croatian Olympic tennis champions.

Rock climbers at Paklenica National Park

One of the highlights of the tennis calendar is in July in Umag when the **Croatian Tennis Open** regularly attracts big names to an event that is becoming more popular every year.

There are also plenty of opportunities to play tennis. Every major coastal resort has tennis courts, and while many are affiliated to hotels, non-residents can also use. The excellent facilities at Umag host the Croatian Tennis Open, but when they are not in use for tournaments or training, they can be rented out, offering a rare chance for amateurs to play at an international tennis venue.

Walking, hiking and climbing

Croatia has lots of opportunities for walking and hiking. The most popular areas with mountaineers and those looking for a real challenge are the **Velebit range** and the sheer limestone walls of **Paklenica National Park**. The park has basic facilities and caters for all levels of climber, from beginner right through to serious mountaineers and daredevil free climbers. At the entrance to the main gorge a steep rock wall is used for practising, training and for showing first-timers the ropes.

Elsewhere, the **Risnjak National Park** at the northern end of Velebit is more suited to those intending to trek and hike. On the eastern edge of the Istrian peninsula, where it meets the Kvarner Gulf, **Mt Učka** is a good option for day trips from the resorts of Opatija and Labin. Southwest of Zagreb are the **Samobor Hills** where Tito first laced up his hiking boots.

Shopping

Croatia is slowly emerging as a good shopping destination, particularly in the bigger cities. **Zagreb** and **Dubrovnik** have a good range of designer stores and interesting shops, with **Split** and other cities catching up fast. Nearly everything is available here that you would find in any other major European city. The towns and villages have smaller outlets selling local produce and handicrafts, and in the coastal resorts the work of local artists is on sale.

What to buy

Food and drink

Croatia produces a lot of food that could be loosely described as 'organic'. Under communism, much of the country's food was produced on a local small-scale or family basis; as a result the people take great pride in the quality and high standard of their produce.

Often the best places to buy the freshest fruit and vegetables are the **bountiful local markets**, still very much alive today despite the increasing number of shopping malls and supermarkets. Most markets in Croatia are open Monday–Saturday 8am–2pm (or longer), and many also work Sunday 8–11am. Markets in the holiday resorts also sell souvenirs, and tend to have extended opening hours.

Food items to look out for are *paški sir*, the excellent salty **sheep's milk cheese** from the North Dalmatian island of Pag, as well as the delicious *pršut* **smoked ham**, which is served in thin slices all along the coastline, but particularly in Dalmatia. Croatian **olive oil** is also highly rated, as are its **truffles**, which are found in the Istrian interior. **Kulen sausage** from Slavonia is a spicy and tasty treat that travels well. On the coast, of course, **fresh fish and seafood** are the highlights, especially the mussels and oysters of places such as Ston and the Lim fjord.

Truffle hunting in Istria

Croatia is also gaining a niche reputation for its **wines**, with a multitude of varieties available. Istria and Dalmatia produce the

TRUFFLES

Istria is the place to be for truffle lovers. The region's interior is one of Europe's most productive regions for truffle hunting. One of the best places to purchase truffle products is Zigante Tartufi, www.zigantetartufi.com. This retail group, which stakes claim to having found the world's biggest truffle, sells its white truffles, black truffles, truffle oil and truffled sheep's milk cheese throughout Istria. They have branches in Motovun, Buje, Buzet, Grožnjan, Koper and Livade, where an excellent restaurant serves truffle dishes (https://restaurantzigante.com).

best known and most highly regarded wines, but family-run and larger vineyards can be found all over the country. Good wine can be expensive but the house wines are mostly very drinkable and good value.

Prošek, a sweet wine, is delicious served with ice and lemon as an aperitif or with desserts. Many Croatians swear by the health-giving powers of the various fruit and herb brandies (*rakija*) that are often also offered before a meal. **Local beers** (Karlovačko and Ožujsko) are popular too; they are every bit as good as more recognized international brands and usually a bit cheaper.

Jewellery and clothes

Items of jewellery, especially **silver pieces and necklaces** made from Adriatic coral, can be found in all of the coastal resorts in summer, sold from small shops or temporary stalls. The jewellery is often made in the outlying villages. Croatia claims to be the original home of the tie, and **handmade silk neckties** (*kravata*) are also popular, as is **lace** from the island of Pag, where the local women have made it by hand for centuries. From Rijeka comes the distinctive traditional *morčić* jewellery.

Designer fashion can be found in Zagreb and Dubrovnik. In Croatia's second city, Split, clothes shopping is a joy. Diocletian's

Palace is a dramatic setting for retail therapy in the many small shops in and around the palace. The citizens of Split are among the best dressed people in the country; though prices are not cheap, quality is high, with bespoke items still good value.

Arts and crafts

Most tourists encounter Croatia's arts and crafts in the coastal resorts in the form of skyline depictions of the historic sights. More interesting are the individual paintings and artworks found in small shops in towns such as Grožnjan and Rovinj.

Where to shop

Zagreb has a multitude of shops selling the latest fashions and designer clothes and a number of modern malls. The heart of the action is on the grand thoroughfare of Ilica and its surrounding streets. Indigo Store (Dežmanova 1; http://indigostore.hr) stocks women's clothes, shoes and accessories, and outlets specializing in Croatian ties, can be found all over Croatia, at airports and major shopping centres.

One of the best places to purchase Croatian wines, *rakija,* olive oil and truffle products is Wine Bar Bornstein (Kaptol 19; www.bornstein.hr), located in a large brick cellar close to the cathedral.

Shopping centres in the capital include Arena Centar (Vice Vukova 6; www.arenacentar.hr), Centar Kaptol (Nova Ves 17; www.centarkaptol.hr), Importanne (Trg Ante Starčevića 7; http://importannecentar.hr) and Emmezeta (Velimira Škorpika 25 and Gospodarska 5; www.emmezeta.hr).

In **Split**, Diocletian's Palace is *the* place to shop, where a number of small domestic designers and international names have their outlets. At the western end of the palace is the shining Marmontova Street that sweeps seawards in a flashy array of European high street stores and trendy boutiques. Shopping is at its busiest during early evening when the local smart set is out to see and be seen. Joker, Split's first shopping mall in the city centre, is near the Hotel Atrium, City Center One is located on Vukovarska Street and there are more opening up just outside the centre.

In **Dubrovnik**, by the Ploče Gate, Maria Boutique sells international designer labels such as Givenchy and Stella McCartney. There are several small, select wine stores, one of the best being Dubrovačka Kuća (Svetog Dominika; tel: 020-322 092), also close to Ploče Gate, and which has an art gallery selling tasteful paintings by local artists.

In **Istria**, Poreč's charming Ulica Decumanus, where Venetian villas brim with tourist shops, is a good place to look for souvenirs and gifts.

Art gallery in Grožnjan

Further north, **Rovinj**'s Ulica Grisia is a pretty street given over to small arts and crafts shops. Arguably the best place to purchase original art in Croatia is in the Istrian hill town of **Grožnjan**, a government-sponsored community of artists.

Trogir is the home of Gena, which makes traditional handmade suits for the smart man in the street as well as Placido Domingo, Goran Ivanišević and Barack Obama.

Nightlife

In the summer months, the Croatian coastline is lively, with smart clubs and stylish cocktail bars vying for trade with the more rustic bars and the omnipresent **summer festivals**. On the coast, things quieten down a bit and many venues close in the winter and often in spring and autumn. Summer can be quiet in inland cities such as Zagreb and Osijek, when most locals escape to the coast.

In **Zagreb** the choice is varied, with live music venues such as *Tvornica Kulture* (www.tvornicakulture.com), clubs like *Boogaloo Club* and *Museum Katran*, super-discos along the lines of *Aquarius*, and prestige jazz haunts like *Boogie Jazz Club*, all a tram ride or walk from the centre.

Outside the capital, other notable nightlife places to go include *Mediterraneo Bar* (Santa Croce 24, **Rovinj**) and *Valentino* (Santa Croce 28; www.valentino-rovinj.com), a fashionable cocktail bar with a waterside terrace. In **Rijeka** look out for *Club Boa* on Ante Starčevića 8 and the club *Život* on Ružićeva 2.

In **Dubrovnik**, *Jazz Caffè Troubadour* (Bunićeva Poljana 2) is a famous jazz bar in the old town. *Culture Club Revelin* (www.club revelin.com) brings top

NOTES

Outdoor nightlife begins in April and culminates in July and August, when festivals offer outdoor cultural entertainment. Makarska, on the mainland, and Novalja on Pag offer most fun for the young.

DJs to its atmospheric club within the Revelin fort, and offers fantastic views from its roof terrace.

In **Split**, nightlife centres on the Diocletian Palace until 11ish, with clubs such as *Vanilla Club* by the Poljud football stadium, and quite a few around Bačvice, taking over after that. **Zadar**, meanwhile, buzzes with bars and clubs such as *The Garden Lounge*, *Arsenal* (http://arsenalzadar.com) and *Bar Ledana* (www.ledana.hr).

Partying in Zagreb

On the islands, **Hvar town** attracts clubbers to *Hula Hula* (www.hulahulahvar.com) and *Kiva*. Pag, meanwhile, has turned itself into the Ibiza of the Adriatic with its mega clubs on Zrće beach in Novalja (summer only).

Culture

There is an extensive cultural programme of theatre, opera and classical music in Zagreb and, to a lesser extent, in the cities of Split, Dubrovnik, Rijeka, Pula, Osijek and Varaždin. In July and August, almost every settlement of any size on the coast has a summer festival. In Dalmatia, you'll hear local folk singing, *klapa*, everywhere but particularly in Omiš, the site of the annual **Klapa Festival**. Korčula is the birthplace of Croatia's traditional sword dance, the **Moreška**, and performances are held in the outdoor theatre in

Korčula Town in high season. The most important Moreška of the year is performed on July 27 on the feast of St Theodore. Contact local tourist offices for more information and tickets.

Croatia for children

In Zagreb, the parks make a good escape for younger travellers. Things are better on the coast, though, where the big resorts have plenty to keep children occupied. The larger hotels have **children's clubs**, especially in Poreč.

The waters of the coast are suitable for children, though look out for rocks and sea urchins. Most beaches are pebbly, so some children might prefer to wear swimming shoes. The **Falconry Centre** and **Etnoland** (www.dalmati.com), both near Šibenik, are very child friendly. The waterpark Istralandia (www.istralandia.hr), near Novigrad in Istria, was Croatia's first and still delivers a fun day out.

Festivals and events

Croatia's cultural scene has received a huge boost since independence, with many old festivals resurrected and others given a new lease of life.

January/February Rijeka Carnival: Croatia's third largest city wakes up from its winter slumber in the days preceding Lent.

February Feast of St Blaise, Dubrovnik: gunpowder, religious processions and marching bands for the feast day of Dubrovnik's patron saint.

Easter Celebrated throughout the country: Vodice, near Šibenik, has an almost week-long celebration of Easter with a number of pageants.

Late May–early June Cest is d'Best, Zagreb: street festival with outdoor performances, sports and events around the capital's main square.

Late June–early July The International Children's Festival, Šibenik: a mixture of ballet, art and performances by children's theatre groups.

Late July–early August Pula Film Festival: there can be few better settings for a film festival than the ancient Roman amphitheatre.
Early July–mid-August Musical Evenings in St Donat's (*Glazbene večeri u Sv. Donatu*), Zadar: the acoustics of this medieval church are perfect for grand classical performances.
Mid-July–late August Dubrovnik Summer Festival (*Dubrovačke Ljetne Igre*): the festival is rapidly establishing a name for itself as one of Europe's top festivals; tickets are limited, but well worth the effort.
July and August Split Summer Festival (*Splitsko Ljeto*): a solid programme of cultural events; many of the performances are in and around Diocletian's Palace. The Summer Events on the Island of Krk: cultural action focuses on Krk Town's old town. Istrian Musical and Cultural Summer: Poreč, Umag, Rovinj, Pula and Grožnjan host cultural events, as do most towns along the Dalmatian coast.
Late September–early October Varaždin Baroque Evenings (*Varaždinske Barokne Večeri*): opera and baroque ensembles.
December St Nicholas Day, Komiža on Vis Island, December 6: In a tradition that dates back many years, local fishermen organize a procession and burn an old wooden boat in honour of the patron saint of sailors. December 24–25: Christmas festivities throughout the country.

Street artist at Cest is d'Best festival

Food and drink

One of the joys of visiting Croatia is its food scene, one of the most undiscovered in Europe. A huge blend of influences reflecting the Balkans' turbulent history, restaurant menus are packed with dishes that have their origins in Turkey, Austria, Hungary and further afield. Local produce features heavily on good restaurants' menus, from Istrian truffles and Pag cheese to Hvar olives and Ston oysters.

With so much coastline, Croatia excels at seafood. Restaurants specializing in fruit de mer are mostly located along the Adriatic coast. Inland Slavonia is a completely different kettle of fish (!) with a more central European feel – think river fish, game, mushrooms and dumplings. Zagreb has the greatest choice of restaurants in the country and is essentially the only place where you will find anything other than local or Italian food of any decent quality.

Top ten things to try

Here we list the top ten things to scoop with a spoon or lance with a fork while holidaying in Croatia:

1. Istrian truffles

The Istrian peninsula is best known in culinary circles for its white and black truffles. Freshly shaved over pasta or scrambled eggs in local taverns, they are a taste sensation.

2. Black risotto (crni rižot)

Made with cuttlefish or squid ink, this strangely black dish from the Dalmatian coast is flavoured with garlic, wine and local olive oil.

3. Pag cheese (paški sir)

This hard sheep's milk cheese from Pag Island has a salty, herbaceous taste – the local sheep graze on the island's wild herbs that grow in salty soil.

4. Fuži with truffle sauce

Traditional Istrian pasta that goes oh-so well with rich, aromatic truffle sauce, a decadent experience.

5. Štrukli

This saltily-sweet dish originated in Zagreb and northern Croatia – it is basically baked oily pastry parcels filled with cottage cheese.

6. Brodet

Fisherman's stew from Dalmatia made with fish, shellfish, tomatoes, and wine, typically served with polenta.

Pag's famous cheese goes well with pršut air-dried ham

7. Peka

A traditional Dalmatian dish of meat or seafood (usually octopus or lamb) slow-cooked with potatoes and vegetables under a bell-like dome covered in embers. The smoky, tender result is unforgettable.

8. Kulen

A spicy, paprika-infused pork sausage from Slavonia, best enjoyed thinly sliced with local bread and cheese.

9. Fritule

Small, sweet doughnuts scented with rum, citrus zest and sometimes raisins, these treats are especially popular during holidays.

10. Rožata

And to finish off your Croatian meal is Dubrovnik's answer to creme caramel, a creamy custard dessert flavoured with local rose liqueur.

When to eat

In the summer season, most restaurants are open all day, though what is on offer often varies depending on the availability of seafood. Traditionally Croatians are early risers, taking a stiff shot of coffee to kick-start the day, perhaps along with a pastry snack. Lunch is usually from noon to 2pm, though this can vary along the coast, where a Mediterranean lifestyle means later lunches and siestas. Dinner is usually eaten later than in most Western

Ispod peke, a traditional octopus meal in Croatia

European countries, with restaurants serving food until 10pm or even later.

Out of season, many restaurants, even in the bigger towns, take a week or two off, or sometimes a couple of months. In the smaller, coastal resorts many close down completely for several months.

What to eat

There is a huge amount of regional variation in Croatia, with seafood the obvious highlight along the coast. In Istria, the Italian influence is strong, whereas in Dalmatia, fish and meat tend to be served with little in the way of sauces. Inland, meat specialities pack menus and richer, stodgier Austrian and Hungarian cooking styles prevail. One common thread is quality, with an emphasis on organic produce and freshness. Fish is usually cooked and eaten on the day it is caught, and all towns and villages have a farmers' market. The fast-food culture and product homogeneity that are found in many other European Union countries have yet to descend on the country. Only pizza can be found everywhere and is usually of a very high quality.

Starters

A common starter in restaurants all over the country is a plate of ham and cheese served with bread. Usually it is the smoked ham known as *pršut*, which is produced in Istria; at its best it is every bit as good as Spain's Serrano ham and Italy's *prosciutto*. The most renowned cheese is *paški sir*, a salty sheep's milk cheese produced on the island of Pag. Ask for a plate of freshly sliced tomatoes as an accompaniment.

Seafood starters are also of high quality. Highlights include *salata od hobotnice* (octopus salad with olive oil), *lignje* (squid) or the more expensive *salata od jastoga* (pieces of lobster marinated in herbs and olive oil). In Slavonia and inland, hearty soups are also common – look out for *fiš paprikaš* from Slavonia, a spicy stew of river fish such as pike, catfish and carp, and *fažol*, a hearty peasant bean stew from Istria. Mushrooms are also used a lot, notably in Istria, which is also the centre of the truffle industry (see page 97).

Fish and seafood

Croatia's range of seafood is extensive. There are numerous highlights, but one inexpensive and unfussy dish that sustains many travellers is seafood risotto, which is both tasty and filling. Croatians like to let their seafood speak for itself, and there are few complicated French-style sauces here. Most dishes come na *žaru* (grilled) or *pećena* (roasted). Most fish is sold by weight and at the top restaurants it will likely be brought out for you to inspect first. Among the bountiful stock in the Adriatic are list (sole), *kovač* (John Dory) and *trilja* (red mullet).

Shellfish are also very popular and of high quality, especially around the Pelješac Peninsula and the town of Ston. Look out for huge *ostrige* (oysters) and *dagnje* (mussels), the latter sometimes coming with a *buzara* sauce. It's reminiscent of *moules marinières* with garlic and white wine, but with a few tomatoes added. *Jastog* (lobster) is expensive compared with other options, but still very good value. The *škampi* (prawns) are often served whole, simply grilled or in a *buzara* sauce.

NOTES

Though not as pronounced as in some of the other Balkan countries, Turkish influences are evident, particularly in indigenous fast food such as meat kebabs and *burek* (cheese or meat baked in filo pastry). Among the desserts, you will also find *baklava*, filo pastry smothered in honey and nuts. Turkish coffee, drunk very strong in tiny cups, is popular.

Meat

In the resorts, meat dishes may be limited to grilled

Shellfish in Istria

beef and pork, but it's not too hard to find delicious spit-roasted meat, usually chicken, veal, beef or lamb, baked with potatoes under a metal bell (*peka*) in hot embers. Between the coast and Zagreb the hills are dotted with small restaurants that specialize in spit-roasted lamb and pork. You can tell which places are open by the pigs and lambs slowly turning over the hot coals outside. This is usually served unadorned and accompanied by bread, potatoes, and a simple salad.

In terms of fast food, the ubiquitous *ćevapčići* is as popular as ever, especially the younger generations. These spicy rissoles are succulent and tasty, and usually come with a salad and bread, making a quick, filling lunch option.

The Austrian influence comes through in the Zagorje region north of the capital, where schnitzels are omnipresent on menus.

Zagreb even has its own version, the *zagrebački odrezak*, which comes stuffed with cheese and ham. In Slavonia, to the east of the capital, the Hungarian influences bring in paprika and hearty stews such as *gulaš*. A highlight here is the fine *kulen* sausage, a large and spicy affair not dissimilar to Spanish chorizo, which is eaten on its own with bread and used in stews.

Desserts

Ice cream (*sladoled*) is superb in Croatia, rivalling Italian *gelati* in its taste and quality. No hot Adriatic summer's day would be complete without at least one, preferably eaten before or after dinner along the waterfront.

Croatian desserts do not stop at ice cream. From the town of Samobor comes *kremšnita*, a creamy and delicate custard cake. *Voćna salata* (fruit salad) is a healthy option, less so are the common *štrudl* (strudel) and *torta* (gateau).

Desserts tend to get more calorific as you head inland, again thanks to the influences of Austria and Hungary. *Palačinke* (pancakes) come laden with cream, nuts and seasonal fruits, although, along the coast, fillings are generally simpler. For the majority of Croatians, though, dessert is usually just a strong cup of coffee, perhaps followed by an ice cream on a postprandial stroll around town.

RESTAURANT CULTURE

There are several kinds of restaurant in Croatia. The first is the formal *restoran*, which are plentiful in the big resorts and cities and usually offer a mix of Croatian and international food. More authentic and more likely to provide regional specialities is a *konoba*, a small family-run restaurant. These often offer dishes of the day and may not even run to a standard menu; the choice varies depending on what is freshest and cheapest at the morning market. The last category is roadside establishments, often called *gostionica*, serving succulent spit-roasted pork and lamb with bread and simple salads.

Market stall puff cakes

Croatian wine

Croatia produces a wide variety of wines of varying quality, from simple table white wines that go with fish dishes, to excellent reds that stand their ground against many wines from France and Italy. Production volumes are such that few bottles make it out of the country. Croatians like to drive out to the vineyards and stock up on supplies in plastic bottles. Istria and the Samobor Hills near Zagreb are packed with small-scale producers selling direct to customers.

Red wines. Dingač from the Pelješac Peninsula in southern Dalmatia is regarded as the king of Croatian wines. This robust fourteen percent wine goes well with all meat dishes and is also very good on its own, although it can be expensive. Pelješac is also home to the considerably cheaper red Plavac, more often than not served as table wine, though certain vintages can also stand on

Liqueurs for sale

their own. Postup is another Pelješac wine and regularly compared to American Zinfandel.

Further north in Dalmatia, Šibenik produces its own Plavina and Babić wines, as well as an acceptable rosé. Neighbouring Primošten produces its own excellent Babić. Although most production in Istria is of white wine, Teran is a passable red, though it can be overloaded with tannin.

White wines. In the north, more than seventy percent of Istria's production is white wine. Look out for Muscatel and Malvazija. In southern Dalmatia, tucked on the end of the Pelješac Peninsula, is the island of Korčula, which is renowned for its Pošip and the especially good Grk, both varieties of white.

It is thought that wine was first produced in Croatia by the Greeks on the island of Vis. Today Vis has myriad vineyards that specialize in

Viški Plavac (red) and Vugava (white), with many small-scale operations. Arguably, the best of all the island wines is Vrbnička Žlahtina. From the vine-covered slopes around Vrbnik, in the north of the Kvarner Gulf island of Krk, this straw-yellow wine is superb and goes particularly well with the local fish dishes; it is also good for drinking on its own on steamy summer nights. A good dessert wine is Prošek, which is the perfect accompaniment to the very sweet desserts and often drunk as an aperitif with ice and lemon.

It is common for locals to dilute their wine with a little water (called a *bevanda*) or add a touch of sparkling mineral water (*gemišt*), with Vrbnička Žlahtina working well in both cases. Connoisseurs may be distressed to see Croatians pouring orange juice into their glasses of red wine, but it actually makes for a very refreshing drink when the temperature rises.

Away from the coast, Slavonia produces some excellent white wines; like the local food, these are very distinctive in character. Two to look out for are Graševina and Kutjevo Chardonnay, which complement the spicy fish dishes of the region.

Other drinks

Beer (*pivo*) is a popular drink, especially in summer. Imported foreign brands are becoming increasingly widespread, but thankfully, there is a good range of domestically owned and produced beers. The best of them all, and commonly available, is Karlovačko, from Karlovac, which has a clean, crisp flavour and a pleasant aftertaste. Its biggest rival is Ožujsko from Zagreb, a heavier tasting Czech-style lager.

Domestic spirits are hugely popular and found in most bars and restaurants. They include the fiery grappa digestif, which can be dynamite, especially if it is home made. *Šljivovica* (plum brandy) is a good digestif, but it can also have quite a kick. Homemade versions tend to be better than that bought from supermarkets. Some infuse *Šljivovica* with herbs and other fruits.

To help you order

Could we have a table for…? **Imate li stol za…?**
Please could you bring...? **Molim vas donesite…?**
The bill, please **Račun molim**
menu **jelovnik**
bread **kruh**
butter **maslac**
coffee **kava**
dessert **desert**
fish **riba**
fruit **voće**
ice cream **sladoled**
lemonade **limunada**
meat **meso**
milk **mlijeko**
mineral water **mineralda voda**
pepper **papar**
rice **riža**
salad **salata**
salt **sol**
sugar **šećer**
tea **čaj**
with milk **s mlijekom**
with lemon **s limunom**
with rum **s rumom**
wine **vino**
white **bijelo**
red **crno**
rosé **roze**

Basic terms

hrana food
jelovnik menu
račun bill
doručak/zajutrak breakfast
gableci/marenda brunch
ručak lunch
večera dinner
tanjur plate
pladanj platter
nož knife
viljuška fork
žlica spoon
čaša glass
šalica cup
dobar tek! bon appetit!
živjeli!/nazdravje! cheers!

Cooking terms

kuhano/lešo boiled
na ražnju spit roasted
na roštilju/na žaru grilled
pečeno fried or roasted
pod pekom baked under a lid
pohani fried in breadcrumbs
prženo fried
u pećnici baked

Menu reader

bakalar cod
banana banana
burek cheese-filled pastry
crna kava black coffee
dagnje mussels
gljive mushrooms
goveđi beef
grah beans
gulaš goulash
hladno pečenje cold meat
hobotnica octopus
ispod peke baked under a cast-iron bell
jabuka apple
jagoda strawberry
jaje egg
janje na ražnju lamb on the spit
jastog lobster
juha soup
kamenica/ostriga oyster
kobasica sausage
kolač cake
kozji sir goat's cheese
krastavac cucumber
krumpir potato
kulen Slavonian sausage
lignje squid
ljuskar shellfish
luk onion
marmelada jam
masline olives
med honey
mineralna voda mineral water
naranča orange
ocat vinegar
omlet sa šunkom ham omelette
palačinke pancakes
pečeni odojak na ražnju roast suckling pig on the spit
pile chicken
pivo beer
pršut Parma ham
rakija brandy
rižot risotto
salata salad
sir cheese
škampi prawns
slag whipped cream
šljivovica plum brandy
stolno vino table wine
šunka ham
sirova raw
kuhana cooked
dimljena smoked
svinjski kotleti pork chops
tartufe truffle
teleći odrezak veal cutlet
umak sauce
voćna salata fruit salad
voćni sok fruit juice
vrhnje cream
zelena paprika green pepper

Places to eat

We have used the following symbols to give an idea of the price for a three-course meal for two people, including a bottle of house wine but excluding tip:

€€€€ = over 100 euros
€€€ = 60–100 euros
€€ = 30–60 euros
€ = under 30 euros

Central and Eastern Croatia

Zagreb

Baltazar Nova Ves 4, 10000 Zagreb, https://baltazar.hr. Barbecued meats served in a rustic dining room in winter and in a courtyard garden in summer (though may be closed during summer). Situated in Gornji Grad, close to the cathedral. **€€€**

BioMania Bistro Ulica Ivana Tkalčića 65, Zagreb 10000, www.biomania.hr. Providing a little respite from the grilled meat served at many establishments across Croatia, *čevapčiči* and tangy cheese can be found at this vegan and vegetarian bolt hole, renowned as one of Europe's best meat- and dairy-free restaurants. **€€**

Heritage Croatian Food Petrinjska ulica 14, Zagreb 10000, www.facebook.com/heritagecroatianfood. Excellent snack bar that specializes in regional cuisine. Only a few tables and madly popular at mealtimes. Most get takeaway. **€**

Vinodol Nikole Tesle 10, 10000 Zagreb, www.vinodol-zg.hr. Vaulted ceilings keep things cosy on cold days in this Donji Grad restaurant, which spills out into a huge courtyard terrace on warmer days. Veal cooked slowly under a peka is one of the specialities, along with veal served with a cheese crust, Zagreb style. **€€**

Osijek

Slavonska Kuća Kamila Firingera 26, 31000 Osijek, www.slavonska-kuca.com. A traditional Slavonian restaurant in the historic Tvrđa, renowned for its spicy fish stew. **€€**

Varaždin

Restoran Angelus Alojzija Stepinca 3, 42000 Varaždin, https://angelus.hr. One of the best restaurants located in the heart of the city. Open daily for lunch and dinner. Great feasts for every Italian food lover. Excellent service and a pleasant atmosphere. **€€**

Istria

Poreč

Gourmet Restaurant Eufrazijeva 26, 52440 Poreč, tel: 052-452 742. This traditional Italian-style pizzeria serves up pizza and pasta dishes on a lively terrace in one of Poreč's most beautiful squares. **€€**

Pizzeria Dali Istarskog razvoda 11, 52440 Poreč, https://pizzeria-dali.eatbu.com. Wood-fired pizzas and pasta dishes are served in this small and traditional restaurant in the heart of town. **€**

Pula

Barkun Krlezhina Ulica 15, 52100 Pula, www.facebook.com/PizzeriaBarkun. Pizzeria in the centre of town, serving good-value pizzas and pasta dishes. **€€**

Scaletta Flavijevska 26, 52100 Pula, www.hotel-scaletta.com. This is a pleasant fine-dining restaurant in the *Scaletta Hotel* close to the amphitheatre, with fish and meat specialities. Try the scampi soup, gnocchi with gorgonzola and excellent fish platter. It also serves lobster for special occasions. **€€€**

Rovinj

Giannino Augusto Ferrija, 38, 52210 Rovinj, https://restoran-giannino.com. *Giannino* serves first-rate fish. It is located in a secluded street away from the main tourist area. **€€**

The Kvarner Gulf

Opatija

Konoba Ribarnica Volosko Andrije Štangera 5, Volosko, 51410 Opatija, tel: 051-701 483. This seafood restaurant, which is extremely popular with the locals, serves delicious, fresh fish every day, alongisde other seafood options. Friendly ambiance. **€€**

The Islands

Konoba Rab Kneza Branimira 3, 51280 Rab, tel: 051-725 666. In the old town, this old-fashioned restaurant serves tasty meat and fish in a cosy dining room. Try *rabska torta* (Rab cake, a local speciality made from almonds) for dessert. **€€€**

Nada Ulica Glavača 22, 51516 Vrbnik, Krk, www.nada-vrbnik.hr. This highly regarded restaurant serves local meat and fish specialities on a large, ambient terrace in the old town. Be sure to try the local Žlahtina white wine, which you can also buy here in presentation boxes to take home.

Pizzeria Draga Braće Vidulića 77, 51550 Mali Lošinj, tel: 051-231 132. Lošinj's favourite pizzeria serves pizza, pasta and salads on a large, covered terrace just one block back from the harbour. **€€**

Dalmatia

Dubrovnik

Lokanda Peskarija Na Ponti bb, 20000 Dubrovnik, www.lokandapeskarija.com. Situated next to the covered fish market in an atmospheric setting overlooking the old harbour, this informal restaurant serves excellent seafood. You know a restaurant is good when it is very popular with locals – but it does mean that reservations are essential for dinner. **€€**

Orhan Od Tabakarije 1, 20000 Dubrovnik, www.restaurant-orhan.com. Just outside the city walls, close to Pile Gate, *Orhan* serves up delicious Dalmatian seafood dishes at outdoor tables overlooking the sea. **€€€**

Sesame Dante Alighieria bb, 20000 Dubrovnik, www.sesame.hr. This charming taverna situated close to the Pile gate serves tasty local specialities; the seafood risotto is particularly good. **€€**

Mali Ston

Kapetanova Kuča 20234 Mali Ston, www.ostrea.hr. This is one of Croatia's top restaurants specializing in oysters and seafood. Try to save room for pudding too, as the gateaux are delicious. Booking ahead recommended.

Makarska

Stari Mlin Prvosvibanjska 43, 21300 Makarska, tel: 021-611 509. Colourful paintings, candles and incense set the mood in this old stone building with a vine-covered terrace. The menu is rather special – Dalmatian seafood dishes plus select Thai specialities. **€€€**

Šibenik

Pelegrini Jurja Dalmatinca 1, 22000 Šibenik, www.pelegrini.hr. A wonderfully located restaurant with outdoor and some indoor tables that have stunning views of the cathedral and over the estuary. Domestic cuisine with an international touch. **€€€**

Split

Galija Tončićeva 12, 21000 Split, www.pizzeriagalija.com. This cosy pizzeria serves some of the city's best pizzas just outside Diocletian's Palace. **€€**

Kod Jože Sredmanuška 4, 21000 Split, tel: 099 352 68 59. All a *konoba* should have: flagstone floor, wooden furniture, great barbecued fish and an endless supply of local wine served by candlelight. **€€**

The Islands

Konoba Adio Mare Marka Pola 2, 20260 Korčula, www.konobaadiomare.hr. A real gem hidden in a narrow side street in the old town. Serves typical Dalmatian meat and fish dishes. **€€**

Konoba pud Brest Milohnići 41, 51511, Milohnići, Krk, www.pud-brest.com. One of the best restaurants on the island of Krk with an eclectic menu of local and national favourites, all eaten around a stone house that was renovated from a ruin by the owners. **€€**

Macondo Groda, 21450 Hvar, www.macondo.com.hr. One of Hvar's best restaurants, situated in a narrow street set back from the main square.

Mali Raj Put Zlatnog rata, 21420 Bol, Brač, http://maliraj-bol.com. Right by the main beach, excellent fish and meat in a lovely setting. **€€€**

Trogir

Alka Augustina Kažotića 15, www.restaurant-alka.hr. One of the longest-established restaurants in Trogir, Alka offers excellent grilled fish and *pašticada* and boasts a very pleasant courtyard. **€€**

Zadar

Foša Kralja Dmitra Zvonimira 2, 23000 Zadar, www.fosa.hr. Traditional fish restaurant located in the former customs house. Enjoy a sumptuous fish platter or fresh spaghetti with clams. **€€**

Lungo Mare Obala kneza Trpimira 23, tel: 091-517 3202. Located on the seafront promenade, this relaxed restaurant serves up a large selection of excellent fresh fish and seafood as well as pastas, risottos and steaks. **€€**

Travel essentials

Practical information

Accessible travel 123
Accommodation 123
Airports 124
Apps 125
Bicycle rental 125
Budgeting 126
Camping 126
Car hire 127
Climate 127
Crime and safety 128
Driving 128
Electricity 130
Embassies and consulates 130
Emergencies 130
Getting there 130
Guides and tours 131
Health and medical care 132
Language 132
LGBTQ+ travellers 134
Money 135
Opening times 135
Police 136
Public holidays 136
Telephones 137
Time zones 137
Tipping 137
Toilets 138
Tourist information 138
Transport 139
Visas and entry requirements 140
Websites and internet access 141

Accessible travel

Many of Croatia's most interesting sights lie within the country's historic old towns, where streets are generally cobbled and buildings are old with narrow staircases, hallways and no lifts, making access for travellers with disabilities somewhat problematic.

Access to beaches can also be difficult, requiring descents over steep steps or crossing rocky outcrops, although the town of Omiš, near Split, has a wheelchair-accessible beach with special ramps to lower people with disabilities into the sea, and the nearby town of Ivašnjak is also wheelchair-accessible.

Travellers with accessible requirements should plan their visits in advance and check with local tourist boards that their needs can be catered for. In general, newly built hotels are more likely to have accessible facilities.

Before travelling, it may be worthwhile to get in contact with the Association of Organizations of Disabled People in Croatia (Zajednica saveza osoba s invaliditetom Hrvatske), www.soih.hr.

Accommodation

Hotels, apartments, campsites and private accommodation in Croatia usually receive a government grade of between one and five stars. Standards in four- and five-star establishments are consistently high, but there are greater variations lower down the accommodation food chain.

Hotels. Croatia offers a wide variety of hotels, from clean and functional resort hotels to luxurious business-oriented establishments and intimate boutique hotels. Hotels in the popular coastal regions fill up quickly for July and August, so book several months in advance. Resorts in high season often demand minimum stays and half-board arrangements, while many close from October to March.

Private accommodation. This ranges from basic rooms to exclusive use of apartments. Book through a travel agent, www.booking.com or www.airbnb.com.

Farmhouses. In Istria, the *Agroturizam* programme offers visitors the opportunity to stay in a family home or a traditional stone farmhouse in the tranquil Istrian hills. Here you can experience a taste of the real Croatia away from the resorts. Further information on the *Agroturizam* programme can be found at www.istra.hr.

Lighthouses. One of the more unusual accommodation options in Croatia comes in the form of renovated but still operational lighthouses. Croatian Lighthouses (www.plovput.hr) can supply information about stays (and online booking) in one of eleven lighthouses located on headlands and islands in Istria and Dalmatia.

Campsites. Croatia also has a large number of campsites called *autocamps*, most of which have good amenities and numerous recreational facilities (see page 126).

I'd like a single/double room **Ja bih jednokrevetnu sobu/ dvokrevetnu sobu**
with bath/shower **sa banjom/tušem**
How much does it cost per night? **Koliko košta za jednu noć?**

Airports

Zagreb international airport (ZAG: www.zagreb-airport.hr) is 17km (12 miles) south of the capital. Pleso Prijevoz (www.plesoprijevoz.hr) operates an efficient shuttle bus between the airport and the city centre. The journey takes 30–45 minutes and costs €8. A taxi into town takes around twenty minutes; fares start at about €20. It is also possible to reach the city by public transportation – ZET bus number 290. It departs every 35 minutes and takes around half an hour.

Croatia's other international airports are:

Split (SPU; www.split-airport.hr) is 20km (12 miles) from the city, journey time thirty minutes; direct buses with Pleso Prijevoz cost €8 each way.

Dubrovnik (DBV; www.airport-dubrovnik.hr) is 18km (11 miles) from the city, journey time twenty minutes; direct shuttle buses with Platanus (https://platanus.hr) cost €10 each way.

Pula (PUY; www.airport-pula.hr) is 7km (4 miles) from the city, journey time

ten minutes; shuttle bus to Pula with Fils (www.fils.hr) costs €8 each way.
Rijeka (RJK; www.rijeka-airport.hr) is 27km (17 miles) from the city, journey time 45 minutes; direct buses with Olivari cost €8 each way.
Osijek (OSI; www.osijek-airport.hr) is 20km (12 miles) from the city, journey time is around fifteen minutes without traffic; transfers cost €5 each way.
Zadar (ZAD; www.zadar-airport.hr) is 11–12km (6–7miles) from the city centre, journey time 15–20 minutes; transfers with Liburnija cost €7 each way (baggage included).

The coastal airports at Pula, Rijeka, Zadar, Split and Dubrovnik are served by regular scheduled and budget flights, with additional routes in summer. Most shuttle buses are timed to coincide with flight arrivals and departures.

Apps

Bolt and **Uber** are predominant taxi apps and available in major cities. **FlixBus** and **Omio** are used for booking tickets for intercity travel. Some cities have their own bus apps, such as **Promet Split**, **Libertas Dubrovnik**, and **ZET Info** for Zagreb. **Explore Croatia** is the official tourism app.

Bicycle rental

It is relatively easy and cheap to hire a bicycle in Croatia, but congested roads and fast traffic can make cycling fairly dangerous in certain areas. The local tourist office is the best source of information about where is the best place to hire a bicycle. Many tourist boards now have special cycling routes with maps available.

Budgeting

Croatia has now become one of the most expensive destinations in Europe so budget accordingly.
Accommodation. A double room with breakfast in a five-star hotel will cost at least €200–400, but you can get a comfortable room in a three-star hotel for around €120. Most hotels have a scale of prices depending on the season. All registered providers of accommodation are obliged to charge tourist tax, a nominal amount.

Meals. The cost of eating out has skyrocketed in recent years but is still just about affordable for most. A three-course meal for two with wine in a decent restaurant costs around €25–40. A simple lunchtime snack, such as grilled meat with bread, salad and mineral water, can cost less than €10. Look out for special lunchtime menus which are considerably cheaper than the evening equivalent.

Nightlife. Alcoholic drinks in Croatia are reasonably priced, with a half-litre of beer costing around €3. The average price for a soft drink or a small bottle of water is about €2–3.

Incidentals. Locally organized day trips start at around €25. Do be aware that charges for museums and attractions vary enormously, with very few free museums to be found. Some will have a nominal charge of about €4, while the charge for others (Dubrovnik's ramparts, for example) can be as high as €40 in the summer.

Camping

Croatia has hundreds of campsites. Many of these cater to a wide range of holidaymakers, including families and naturists. Many sites offer extensive land- and water-based sporting activities. Most campsites are only open from April to October, some just July and August.

Approximately ninety percent of the campsites lie along the Adriatic coast and on the surrounding islands. The best-equipped and most highly organized sites are found in the regions of Istria and Kvarner in the north. For those who really want to escape modern-day living, the most memorable sites are in Dalmatia. Koversada in Vrsar, Istria, is one of the biggest and the oldest naturist campsite in Europe.

For a list of campsites, contact the Croatian Camping Union at www.camping.hr.

Car hire

International and local car-hire companies operate throughout Croatia. Drivers must be over 21 years old (although some allow younger drivers for an extra charge) and have held a valid driving licence for a minimum of one or two years. A credit/debit card and a current passport or national identity card are also required for car hire.

Basic insurance is included in the price, but it is advisable to purchase Collision Damage Waiver (CDW) and Theft Protection (TP) for the duration of the hire. Accidents must be reported to the police (tel: 112) immediately, otherwise the insurance is void.

Prices for a weekly economy rental (such as a Toyota Yaris) vary widely, but can start at about €50 in mid to high season.

I want to rent a car **Želim iznajmiti auto**
tomorrow **sutra**
for one day/one week **na jedan dan/jednu sedmicu**
Please include full insurance **Molim vas uključite kasko osiguranje**

Climate

The best time to visit Croatia is during late spring, summer and early autumn when days are sunny and dry. Coastal temperatures regularly reach 30°C (86°F) in August. The Croatian coast is significantly warmer than its interior in winter. In January, temperatures in the east of the country can fall as low as -5°C (23°F) but can be as high as 10°C (50°F) in Istria. Autumn, although mild, can be wet. The temperature chart that follows is for Croatia's capital city, Zagreb.

	J	F	M	A	M	J	J	A	S	O	N	D
min												
°C	-4	-3	2	5	9	13	15	14	11	7	3	-1
°F	24	27	36	41	48	55	59	57	52	45	37	30
max												
°C	3	6	11	16	21	24	27	26	23	16	8	5
°F	37	43	52	61	70	75	81	79	73	61	46	41

Crime and safety

Crime rates in Croatia are lower than those in many European countries and crimes against tourists are rare occurrences. However, as in any other country, visitors should use their common sense: carry personal belongings securely; do not leave valuables in unattended vehicles or on the beach; don't stop if someone tries to flag you down on the roadside, and avoid walking alone at night in poorly lit areas.

If you are a victim of crime, call the emergency services, tel: 112. Uncleared land mines pose a risk only in isolated areas and are usually signed. However, do not stray from roads, public areas or established paths without a qualified guide.

Driving

As in the rest of Continental Europe, people drive on the right in Croatia. Motorways run between Zagreb and along much of the coast, but traffic jams caused by slow-moving vehicles remain a common problem on single lane roads and in hotspots on the motorways during peak summer weekends.

Road conditions. Croatia's motorway network has a toll system and the roads are in a good condition. Road surfaces on many other main routes are also good, with frequent passing places.

Rules and regulations. To drive your own vehicle in Croatia you will need a valid driving licence, registration documents and Green Card insurance (for non-EU registered vehicles). Speed limits are 50kmh (31mph) in residential areas, 90kmh (55mph) outside residential areas, 110kmh (68mph) on motorways and 130kmhr (80mph) on freeways. With limited exceptions, when 0.5 percent is permissible, there is zero tolerance on alcohol consumption for drivers. As is standard in many other countries, it is compulsory to wear seat belts and mobile phones should not be used while driving. Headlights should be switched on at all times while driving during the daylight-saving period (October to March). Check the detailed regulations for requirements for snow chains, hazard warnings, spare bulbs and safety equipment.

autobusna stanica bus stop
križanje crossroads/crossing
opasan zavoj/opasan krivina dangerous bend/dangerous curve
opasnost danger
parkiranje dozvoljeno/zabranjeno parkiranje parking permitted/no parking
pažnja, radovi men working
pješaci pedestrians
slijepa ulica no through road (dead end)
stani halt
stop stop
strm uspon steep hill
vozi na desnoj/lijevoj strani drive on the right/left
vozi oprezno drive with care
zabranjen ulaz no entry
zaobilaznica detour
Are we on the right road for…? **Je li ovo cesta za…?**
Fill the tank, please, with… **Napunite spremnik goriva, molim, sa…**
My car's broken down. **Auto mi se pokvarilo.**
There's been an accident. **Dogodila se prometna nesreća.**

The police must be informed immediately about traffic accidents (tel: 112). Violations like speeding can incur an on-the-spot fine.

Parking. Car parks, often located just outside the pedestrianized old towns, cost €1–2 an hour. Fees are often charged 24 hours a day, seven days a week. In some places the arrival of a tow-away truck can be very swift.

If you need help. The Croatian Automobile Club (Hrvatski Autoklub – hak) provides emergency breakdown assistance (tel: 1987; www.hak.hr). Calls should be prefixed 01 if made from a mobile telephone.

Road signs. Generally use internationally recognized pictographs.

Electricity

The standard current is 230-volt, 50Hz. Plugs have two round pins.

Embassies and consulates

A number of countries have consulates in Split and Dubrovnik; embassies are located in the capital, Zagreb:

Australia: Grand Centar, 5th floor, Hektoroviceva 2; tel: 01-489 1200; www.croatia.embassy.gov.au.

Canada: Prilaz Gjure Deželića 4; tel: 01-488 1200; www.international.gc.ca/

Ireland: Trg Žrtava Fašizma 1; tel: 01-627 8920; https://www.ireland.ie/en/croatia/zagreb/.

South Africa: (Honorary consulate) Vinkovićeva 7; tel: 01-468 0981; www.dirco.gov.za.

UK: Ivana Lučića 4; tel: 01-600 9100; www.gov.uk/world/croatia.

US: Thomasa Jeffersona 2; tel: 01-661 2200; https://hr.usembassy.gov.

Most embassies and consulates are open Mon–Fri 8 or 9am–4 or 5pm, and close for an hour at lunchtime.

Emergencies

Dial 112 for all emergency services.

Getting there

Croatia's national airline (www.croatiaairlines.com) and its partners connect the country with most major European cities, including London, Paris, Rome, Vienna, Brussels, Zurich and Munich. British Airways (www.britishairways.com) has direct flights from London Heathrow to Zagreb and London Heathrow and London Gatwick to Split and from London Heathrow to Dubrovnik. EasyJet (www.easyjet.com) covers much of the country, with flights from London Gatwick to Pula and Dubrovnik; from London Luton to Pula and Split; Manchester to Dubrovnik and Split; Glasgow to Split and Pula; Bristol to Dubrovnik, Pula and Split; and Liverpool to Split.

Jet2 (www.jet2.com) has flights from Birmingham, Manchester and Stansted to Pula. Ryanair (www.ryanair.com) has myriad flights from various UK airports (even to Osijek) and Wizz Air (www.wizzair.com) flies from London Luton to Split, Zagreb and Dubrovnik.

Most other airlines include options with indirect flights to Zagreb, Dubrovnik, Split, Rijeka, Pula and Zadar via Germany or other locations in Europe. Compare flights and find deals with www.skyscanner.net, www.kayak.com, www.google.com/flights and www.momondo.com. Flight times are about 2.5 hours, and air fares vary significantly from season to season, often rising to extortionate heights during the summer if not booked well in advance. Note that many of the carriers operate seasonal flights only.

Guides and tours

Escorted coach tours are a popular way to see Croatia, as are guided walking tours of cities and towns. Local travel agents and tourist offices can arrange either of these.

One of the biggest operators with branches throughout Croatia is **Kompas** (https://kompas-travel.com). At the other end of the scale, niche operators such as **Secret Dalmatia** (www.secretdalmatia.com), **Regent Holidays** (www.regent-holidays.co.uk) and **Original Travel** (www.original travel.co.uk) have opened up less discovered secrets of Croatia to visitors.

Local travel agencies can provide visitors with information about one-day or longer guided tours and excursions, as well as information on specialist activities such as sailing, shooting, fishing, climbing, horse riding and adventure sports.

Health and medical care

It is safe to drink tap water throughout Croatia, and visitors do not require any inoculations to travel here. The most common health problems experienced by visitors are the result of sunstroke, sunburn and dehydration, sometimes exacerbated by too much alcohol.

During summer insect repellent is recommended, as is the wearing of beach/diver's shoes when swimming in rocky areas, because of spiny sea urchins. Contact with these is painful and could require medical attention.

The UK and many European countries have an agreement with Croatia that offers their citizens free medical care. Before travelling, UK citizens should apply for a free UK Global Health Insurance Card (GHIC) online at https://www.nhs.uk/using-the-nhs/healthcare-abroad/apply-for-a-free-uk-global-health-insurance-card-ghic/. If you currently hold a European Health Insurance Card (EHIC), it will remain valid until the expiry date on the card. It is recommended that all visitors take out private travel insurance to cover any unforeseen medical expenses. Local tourist offices have lists of doctors, medical centres, hospitals, dentists and pharmacies (called an *apoteka* or *ljekarna*, usually with large green cross).

Where's the nearest (all-night) pharmacy? **Gdje je najbliža apoteka (24-satna)**
I need a doctor/dentist **Trebao bih liječnika/zubara**
hospital **bolnica**
an upset stomach **boli me želudac**
sunburn/a fever **opekotina od sunca/groznica**

Language

Pronunciation is regular and easy. The accents on letters are important – c is a different letter from č and pronounced very differently, and lj is a 'letter' in its own right. Below are some guidelines where pronunciation of letters differs from English.

a like the 'a' in 'cat'
c like the 'ts' in 'hats'
č like the 'ch' in 'chink'
ć like the 'tch' in 'catch'
dž like the 'j' in 'judge'
e like the 'e' in 'fell'
g like the 'g' in 'golf'
h a guttural sound like the 'ch' in 'loch'
i like the 'ee' in 'yippee'
j like the 'y' in 'yahoo'

k like the 'c' in 'cap'
lj like the 'll' in 'millionaire'
nj like the 'ny' in canyon
o like the 'o' in 'tot'
r always 'rolled'
s like the 's' in 'sing'
š like the 'sh' in 'shine'
u like the 'oo' in 'moo'
z like the 'z' in 'crazy'
ž like the 's' in 'pleasure'

good morning/afternoon/evening **dobro jutro/dan/večer**
goodbye **do viđenja**
please **molim**
thank you **hvala**
Excuse me **oprostite**
yesterday/today/tomorrow **jučer/danas/sutra**
day/week/month/year **dan/tjedan/mjesec/godina**
where/when/how **gdje/kada/kako**
Is this the road to...? **Je li ovo cesta za...?**
how long/how far? **koliko dugo/koliko daleko?**
left/right **lijevo/desno**
cheap/expensive **jeftin/skup**
hot/cold/warm **vruće/hladno/toplo**
old/new **star/nov**
open/closed **otvoreno/zatvoreno**
vacant/occupied **prazan/zauzet**
early/late **rano/kasno**
What does this mean? **Što ovo znači?**
I don't understand **Ne razumijem**
I don't know **Ne znam**
Can you write it down **Možete li mi to zapisati?**

Help me, please **Molim vas pomozite mi**
Get a doctor, quickly! **Trebam doktora brzo!**
Pleased to meet you **Drago mi je**
How are you? **Kako ste?**
Very well thank you, and yourself? **Dobro hvala, a vi?**

Days
Sunday **nedjelja**
Monday **ponedjeljak**
Tuesday **utorak**
Wednesday **srijeda**
Thursday **četvrtak**
Friday **petak**
Saturday **subota**
What day/date is today? **Koji je danas dan/datum?**

LGBTQ+ travellers

Homosexuality has been legal in Croatia since 1977; however, being LGBTQ+ is tolerated instead of widely accepted. There are still some who will take offence at public displays of affection, particularly in rural areas. In touristy places sharing a hotel room should not be an issue, though, and a limited LGBTQ+ scene exists in cities and resorts such as Zagreb, Dubrovnik, Rovinj and Hvar. See www.balconn.com for listings and advice. Zagreb Pride (www.zagreb-pride.net) has been annually held since 2005.

Money

Currency. Since January 2023, the Croatian currency has been the euro.
Currency exchange. Normal banking hours are Mon–Fri 8/9am–3/4pm and often closed on weekends, some are open on Sat between 8am–noon. Currency can also be exchanged in exchange offices, hotels and at

any post office counter. You must take your passport.

ATMs. Cashpoints are readily available and debit cards carrying the Maestro, MasterCard, Visa, Cirrus and Plus symbols are widely accepted.

Credit cards. Credit card cash advances can be withdrawn from ATMs and standard international credit cards are accepted everywhere.

Can I pay with this credit card? **Primate li kreditne kartice?**
I want to change some pounds/dollars **Želim promijeniti engleske funte/američke dolare**
Can you cash a traveller's cheque? **Možete li mi unovčiti putni ček?**
Where's the nearest bank/currency exchange office? **Gdje je najbliža banka/mjenjačnica?**
How much is that? **Koliko ovo košta?**

Opening times

Business hours are generally Mon–Fri 8am–4pm. Banks are open Mon–Fri 8/9am–3/4pm and usually closed on weekends. Shops and department stores in Croatia usually open Mon–Sat 8/9am–8/9pm, some close earlier on Sat. In the resorts shops often open Mon–Fri 8am–1pm, close for the afternoon and open again in the evening, 5–11pm.

Some larger towns have a 24-hour pharmacy and some have 24-hour grocery shops. Café-bars usually open daily 7am–midnight and most restaurants open from midday to midnight. Museum opening times vary considerably and they are often closed on Monday.

Many Croatian towns and resorts have a fresh food market and a general market. Guide opening times are Mon–Sat 7/8am–2pm; some also open Sun 8–11am. Markets selling souvenirs often have longer opening hours.

Note that family run businesses and smaller museums may often vary their opening times considerably, according to the season and often at short notice, because of individual circumstances or their judgement of the likelihood of tourist business.

Police

Croatian police wear dark blue uniforms and are generally helpful and friendly; some speak English.

Anyone involved in a road traffic accident is legally required to report it to the police and not to move the vehicle unless it is causing danger or an obstruction. In the case of emergency, tel: **112**.

Where's the nearest police station? **Gdje je najbliža policijska stanica?**
I've lost my wallet/bag/passport **Izgubio sam novčanik/torbu/putovnicu**

Public holidays

The following is a list of the national holidays in Croatia:
January 1 *Nova Godina* (New Year's Day)
January 6 *Sveta tri kralja* (Epiphany)
May 1 *Međunarodni Praznik Rada* (Labour Day)
June 22 *Dan antifašističke borbe* (Anti-Fascist Resistance Day)
June 25 *Dan Državnosti* (Croatian National Day)
August 5 *Dan Pobjede i Dan Domovinske Zahvalnosti* (Victory Day and National Thanksgiving Day)
August 15 *Velika Gospa* (Feast of the Assumption)
October 8 *Dan Nezavisnosti* (Independence Day)
November 1 *Dan Svih Svetih* (All Saints' Day)
December 25–26 *Božićni blagdani* (Christmas)
Movable dates:
Uskrs (Easter)
Corpus Christi (Corpus Christi)

Telephones

Croatia's country code is 385. When calling from overseas the initial 0 in the local area code should not be dialled. Mobile phone numbers begin

09 and all the digits must be dialled.

Mobile phone coverage is extensive throughout the country, but with patchy coverage in some of the mountainous hinterland. Call and data charges are the same as in other EU countries, but for longer stays you might want to buy a local SIM card. While 4G and 5G are spreading around the country, there are still inland areas where there is not even 3G and you won't be able to receive data.

Can you get me this number? **Možete li molim vas nazvati ovaj broj?**
Reverse charge (collect) **naplatite osobi koju zovem**
Personal call **osobni poziv**

Time zones

Croatia operates GMT+1, and is one hour ahead of the UK, six hours ahead of New York, the same as Johannesburg, eight hours behind Sydney and ten hours behind Auckland. Clocks go forward one hour between April and October.

Tipping

Hotel and restaurant bills usually include tax and service in the form of a cover charge (called a *couvert*), but it is customary to leave ten percent. If you find the service particularly wonderful you can tip fifteen percent. Taxi drivers in the bigger cities sometimes round up the fare, so an additional tip is not always needed.

Toilets

Toilets (*toalet* or WC) are usually marked *muški* for men and *ženski* for women.

Tourist information

The Croatian National Tourist Board (Hrvatska Turistička Zajednica) has offices in many countries. You can visit their website www.croatia.hr.

UK: Dawson House, 5 Jewry Street, Office 213, Fenchurch, London EC3N 2EX; e-mail: info@croatia-london.co.uk.

USA: 33 Irving Pl, New York 1003; e-mail: info.US@croatia.hr.

There are local tourist offices throughout Croatia:

Baška: Kralja Zvonimira 114; www.visitbaska.hr.

Bol: Porat Bolskih Pomoraca bb; www.bol.hr.

Dubrovnik: Brsalje 5; www.tzdubrovnik.hr.

Grožnjan: Umberta Gorjana 3; www.coloursofistria.com.

Hvar: Trg Svetog Stjepana 42; https://visithvar.hr.

Korčula Town: Trg 19. travnja 1921 br. 40; www.visitkorcula.eu.

Krk Town: Vela Placa 1; www.visitkrk.city.

Makarska: Franjevački put 2; www.makarska-info.hr.

Mali Lošinj: Priko 42; www.visitlosinj.hr.

Motovun: Trg Andrea Antico 1; http://tz-motovun.hr.

Opatija: Maršala Tita 128; www.visitopatija.com.

Osijek: Županijska 2; www.tzosijek.hr.

Poreč: Zagrebačka 9; www.myporec.com.

Pula: Forum 3; www.pulainfo.hr.

Rab: Trg Municipium Arba 8; www.rab-visit.com.

Rijeka: Korzo 14; https://visitrijeka.hr.

Rovinj: Trg na mostu 2; www.rovinj-tourism.com.

Šibenik: Fausta Vrančića 18; www.sibenik-tourism.hr.

Split: Obala Hrvatskog Narodnog Preporoda 9; www.visitsplit.com.

Trogir: Trg Ivana Pavla II/1; www.visittrogir.hr.

Varaždin: Ivana Padovca 3; www.visitvarazdin.hr.

Zadar: Jurja Barakovića 5; www.zadar.hr.

Zagreb: Trg Bana Josipa Jelačića 11; www.infozagreb.hr.

There are also tourist offices in many of Croatia's National Parks:

Brijuni: Brionska 10, 52212 Fažana; www.np-brijuni.hr.

Kornati: Rudina bb, 22243 Murter; www.tzo-murter.hr.

Krka: Trg Ivana Pavla II 5, 22000 Šibenik; www.np-krka.hr.

Mljet: Pristanište 2, 20226 Govedari; www.np-mljet.hr.

Paklenica: Dr Franje Tuđmana 14a, 23244 Starigrad Paklenica; https://np-paklenica.hr.
Plitvice National Park: Josipa Jovića 19, 53231 Plitvička Jezera; www.np-plitvicka-jezera.hr.
Risnjak: Bijela Vodica 48, 51317 Crni Lug; http://np-risnjak.hr.
Sjeverni (North) Velebit: Krasno 96, 53274 Krasno; www.np-sjeverni-velebit.hr.

Transport

Buses. Croatia has an extensive local and national bus network. Tickets for local services should be bought from the driver, through an app or from a machine. Services generally operate daily 4am–11pm though in smaller towns and villages there may be no Sunday service.

Arriva (www.arriva.com.hr) is the main operator for long distance services. Tickets can be purchased online, through Arriva Croatia free mobile app, from the local bus station or on-board. National bus services can be boarded at the bus stations or hailed at a designated stop. For information on long distance internal services, see www.akz.hr.

Taxis. Uber only operates in Zagreb, Split and Dubrovnik. In smaller places you will have to take a local taxi.

Trains. Rail travel is slow, with few direct connections between major towns and cities, and most Croatians do not travel by train. Tickets are cheap and can be purchased from railway stations or the onboard conductor. For train information, visit www.hzpp.hr.

Trams. The cities of Zagreb and Osijek both have tram services that operate a similar timetable to the bus services. Tram tickets should be purchased from a tobacco kiosk and passengers have to validate tickets in the onboard machines.

By air. Regular domestic flights operated by Croatia Airlines connect Zagreb to Dubrovnik, Lošinj, Osijek, Pula, Brač, Split and Zadar and some of the latter to each other in season (Split–Osijek, for instance).

By ferry. Jadrolinija (www.jadrolinija.hr) is the main car and passenger ferry operator in Croatia, with numerous routes along the Dalmatian coast and between the mainland and the islands.

Tickets must be purchased online or from the ticket office near the ferry dock prior to departure. In the summer months it is advisable to arrive in good time and buy vehicle tickets well in advance to minimize the risk of waiting in lengthy traffic queues to board a ferry. Foot passengers can usually purchase tickets just before their departure.

Where can I get a taxi? **Gdje ima taksija?**
What's the fare to…? **Koliko košta za…?**
When's the next bus to…? **Kada polazi slijedeći autobus za…?**
I want a ticket to… **Želim kartu za…**
single/return **u jednom smjeru/povratna**
Will you tell me when to get off? **Možete mi reći kad je moja stanica?**

Visas and entry requirements

Any non-EU national entering Croatia must possess a valid passport (EU citizens may enter using their national ID card). For stays of less than ninety days, citizens of EU countries, the UK, the USA, Canada, Australia and New Zealand can enter Croatia without a visa. South Africans need a visa to visit Croatia.

Visitors to Croatia are required to register with the local police in each town or resort that they stay in, even if visiting friends or relatives. Hotels, campsites and travel agencies offering private accommodation automatically register guests. If you fail to register you may experience difficulties if you need to report anything to the police.

The **Consular Department of the Croatian Foreign Ministry** (tel: 01-456 9964; www.mvep.gov.hr) can provide further information, including a list of nationalities that require a visa to enter Croatia.

Currency restrictions. Foreign currency can be taken freely in and out of the country, but amounts over €10,000 must be declared.

Customs allowances. Visitors from other parts of the European Union have no limits on what they can import, as long as they can prove it is for personal use. Visitors from outside the EU can bring 4 litres of wine, 1 litre of spirits, 60 millilitres of perfume and 200 cigarettes without any duty being paid.

I've nothing to declare **Nemam ništa za prijaviti**
It's for my personal use **Ovo su moje stvari**

Websites and internet access

Most newer hotels provide free Wi-Fi, although a few insist on a charge. Many cafés and restaurants offer free Wi-Fi. Good websites for getting information before you go include the following:

www.croatia.hr. The Croatian National Tourist Board provides lots of useful information, with details about accommodation, transport, national parks, current events, as well as an updated weather report.

https://vlada.gov.hr. The homepage of the Republic of Croatia contains general information about the country.

www.visit-croatia.co.uk. Provides information about Croatia and its different regions. The site also has links to other useful websites and links to UK tour operators offering holidays in Croatia.

www.camping.hr. The homepage of the Croatian Camping Union includes a useful contact number for prospective campers.

Index

Đakovo 48

B
Baška 66
Biograd 73
Biševo 88
Borik 73
Brač 85
  Bol 85
  Hermitage Blaca 85
  Žlatni Rat 85
Brela 79
Brijuni Islands 58
Buzet 60

C
Cavtat 84
children 102
Cres Town 68
culture 101

D
Dalmatia 69
diving 91
Drvenik 79
Dubrovnik 79
  cathedral 83
  medieval walls 81
  Pile Gate 81
  Ploče Gate 81
  Rector's Palace 83

E
Elaphite Islands 89
Etnoland 73

F
football 93

G
Grožnjan 60

H
Homeland War Museum 84
Hum 61
Hvar 86

I
Istria 51

K
Kaštela 77
Kopački rit Nature Park 48
Korčula 88
  Korčula Town 88
  Marco Polo House 89
  St Mark's Cathedral 89
Kornati Islands National Park 75
Krapanj 75
Krapinske Toplice 46
Krk 66
Krka National Park 74
Kvarner Gulf 61

L
Labin 57
Lake Jarun 44
Limski Zaljev 58
Lokrum 84
Lošinj 68
Lovran 65

M
Makarska 79
Makarska Riviera 79
Mali Lošinj 68
Mljet 89
  Mljet National Park 89
  St Mary's Island 89
money 135
Motovun 59

N
Novalja 67
Novigrad 57

O
Omiš 78
Opatija 64
Opatija Riviera 63
Osijek 47, 48

P
Pag 67
Pag Town 67
Paklenica National Park 65
Pazin 58
Pelješac Peninsula 79
Plitvice Lakes National Park 47
Podgora 79
Poreč 56
  Basilica of Euphrasius 56
  Romanesque House 56
Prvić 75
Pula 51
  Cathedral of St Mary 53
  Roman Amphitheatre 51
  Roman Forum 52
  Temple of Augustus 52
  Triumphal Arch of Sergius 52

R

Rab 67
Rabac 57
Rijeka 62
  Our Lady of Trsat church 63
  Stari Grad 63
  St Vitus 63
  Trsat castle 63
Roški Slap 75
Rovinj 53
  Grisia 55
  Heritage Museum 54
  Rovinj Aquarium 54
  St Euphemia 53

S

sailing 92
Salona 77
Senj 65
shopping 95
Šibenik 72
  Falconry Centre 73
  garden of St Lawrence's Monastery 72
  Šibenik Cathedral 72
Skradin 75
Skradinski Buk 75
Slavonia 47
Solaris 73
Šolta 86
Split 76
  Bačvice 77
  Cathedral of St Domnius 76
  Diocletian's Palace 76
  Golden Gate 76
  Marmontova 77
  Meštrović Gallery 76
  Split Gallery of Modern Art 76
  Zenta 77
Ston 79

T

tennis 94
Trakošćan Castle 45
Trogir 73
  cathedral 74
  Čipiko Palace 74
  Kamerlengo Castle 74
Tučepi 79
Tvrđa 49

U

Učka Mountains 65
Umag 57

V

Varaždin 44
Veliki Tabor 46
Veli Lošinj 68
Vis 86
  Komiža 87
  Maritime Museum 87
  Vis Town 87
Visovac 75
Vodice 73
Vodnjan 53
Volosko 65
Vrsar 56
Vukovar 49

W

walking, hiking and climbing 95
watersports 93
where to shop 98

Z

Zadar 70
  Archaeological Museum 71
  Narodni Trg 70
  Široka Ulica 70
  St Donat's Church 70
  St Simeon church 70
  Town Loggia 70
  Zadar Cathedral 71
  Zadar Museum of Antique Glass 71
Zagorje 44
Zagreb 35
  Art Pavilion 36
  Atelier Meštrović 42
  Botanical Gardens 44
  Dolac Market 40
  Lisinski Concert Hall 43
  Lotršćak Tower 40
  Maksimir Park 44
  Mimara 38
  Museum of Arts and Crafts 37
  Museum of Broken Relationships 41
  Museum of Contemporary Art 43
  National Library 43
  statue of King Tomislav 36
  St Mark's Church 41
  Strossmayer Gallery 36
  Tkalčićeva 42
  Trg bana Josipa Jelačića 38
  Zagreb Cathedral 39
  Zagreb City Museum 42
  Zagreb Zoo 44
Zaostrog 79
Zlarin 75

MINI
CROATIA

Second edition 2025

Editor: Libby Davies
Author: Marc Di Duca
Picture Editor: Piotr Kala
Picture Manager: Tom Smyth
Cartography Update: Katie Bennett
Layout: Claire Armstrong
Production Operations Manager: Katie Bennett
Publishing Technology Manager: Rebeka Davies
Head of Publishing: Sarah Clark
Photography Credits: All images Shutterstock and iStock except: Bigstock 10, 42, 57; Christian Maréchal/Wikimedia Commons under CC BY 3.0 license 31; Corrie Wingate/Apa Publications 9, 16BR, 40, 41, 46, 59, 88, 99, 109; Dominic Burdon/Apa Publications 14CL, 16CL, 37, 49, 51, 52, 71, 77, 78, 81; Gregory wrona/Apa Publications 105; Mario Romulić & Dražen Stojčić/Croatian National Tourist Board 92; Public domain 25
Cover Credits: Visovac monastery from above in Krka National Park **iStock**

About the author

Marc Di Duca has been a full-time travel guide author for over two decades, during which he has contributed to almost 200 guides to destinations as diverse as Siberia, Brazil and the Caribbean for all major travel publishers. Based in the Czech Republic, Marc is a regular visitor to the Balkans where hiking in the remote and largely undiscovered mountains of Northern Albania comes a close second to lounging on the beaches of the Adriatic as his favourite activity.

Distribution

UK, Ireland and Europe: Apa Publications (UK) Ltd; mail@roughguides.com
United States and Canada: Two Rivers; ips@ingramcontent.com
Australia and New Zealand: Woodslane; info@woodslane.com.au
Worldwide: Apa Publications (UK) Ltd; mail@roughguides.com

MIX
Paper from responsible sources
FSC® C014138

Special Sales, Content Licensing and CoPublishing

Rough Guides can be purchased in bulk quantities at discounted prices. We can create special editions, personalized jackets and corporate imprints tailored to your needs.
mail@roughguides.com
roughguides.com

EU Representative

LOGOS EUROPE, 9 rue Nicolas Poussin, 17000, LA ROCHELLE, France; Contact@logoseurope.eu; +33 (0) 667937378

Printed by Finidr in Czech Republic

ISBN: 9781835293928

This book was produced using **Typefi** automated publishing software.

A catalogue record for this book is available from the British Library

Contact us

Every effort has been made to ensure that this publication is accurate, free from safety risks, and provides accurate information. However, changes and errors are inevitable. The publisher is not responsible for any resulting loss, inconvenience, injury or safety concerns arising from the use of this book. If you notice any errors, outdated information, or potential safety risks, please send your comments with the subject line "Rough Guide Mini Croatia Update" to mail@roughguides.com.